fantastic federer

fantastic federer

Chris Bowers

JOHN BLAKE

Published by John Blake Publishing Ltd,
3 Bramber Court, 2 Bramber Road,
London W14 9PB, England

www.blake.co.uk

First published in hardback in 2006

ISBN 1 84454 278 5

British Library Cataloguing-in-Publication Data:

A catalogue record for this book is available from the British Library.

Design by www.envydesign.co.uk

Printed in Great Britain by Creative Print and Design, Wales

1 3 5 7 9 10 8 6 4 2

Papers used by John Blake Publishing are natural, recyclable products
made from wood grown in sustainable forests. The manufacturing processes
conform to the environmental regulations of the country of origin.

On Sunday, 6 July 2003, Roger Federer finally won the most prestigious prize in tennis: the Wimbledon men's singles title. Following his victory, a journalist for Swiss radio soon ran out of adjectives to describe Federer's superb displays in beating Andy Roddick and Mark Philippoussis in the final two rounds. Ultimately, he simply succumbed to the emotion of the moment and screamed into his microphone, 'Fantastisch! Fantastisch! Fantastisch!'

About The Author

Chris Bowers is a freelance writer and broadcaster who has covered the global tennis circuit since 1992. After graduating in German with History, Linguistics and Music in 1983, he trained as a newspaper journalist before moving into radio in 1986. Over the next two years, he spent twenty-two months working for Switzerland's overseas radio service, Swiss Radio International, in Bern. During that time he played a year's Swiss-league tennis for the Flamingo tennis club – owned by Frantisek Kratochvil, whose son Michel became a touring professional – where his doubles partner was Severin Lüthi, who is now captain of the Swiss Davis Cup team. After working for an environmental organisation for two years, he went full-time on the global tennis tour in 1992, working for newspapers, magazines, radio, television and internet media. He is best known as a commentator for BBC Radio Five Live, BBC World Service and Eurosport, and he also writes regularly for *The Times*, the *Observer* and the *Independent*. This is his fourth book about tennis. He is forty-five years old and lives with his partner and daughter in East Sussex, England.

Introduction

It's often difficult to recognise legends or all-time greats when they're at the height of their powers. It frequently takes the decline in their careers for people to realise the enormity of what they have achieved.

Roger Federer defies this phenomenon. When people watch him play tennis, they know that, even at just twenty-four, he's something special. Not only something special, but also someone who is universally liked among those who deal with him. Indeed, it's almost impossible to find anyone with a bad word to say about him, and one highly experienced tennis official who has been dealing with player–media liaison for nearly twenty years described him as being 'not only the nicest number one I have ever dealt with but the nicest player I have ever dealt with'.

Roger Federer isn't someone from the gutter of a ghetto who has defied all obstacles to reach the top. He's no middle-class rebel without a cause who turned his anger into on-court intensity. Unlike players like Jimmy Connors, Lleyton Hewitt and even Pete Sampras, Federer doesn't turn his opponent into a deeply hated enemy for the duration of a match. With him, it isn't personal; he just wants to play better than his opponent, to win the last point – and, if possible, to win it in style.

So what makes up the character and psyche of Roger Federer, the second child of a modestly affluent but unremarkable middle-class family from Basel? That is the essence of this book.

I first approached Roger and his entourage (unlike almost all top players, Roger is managed as much by his family as by an agency) in early 2004 to ask if he and I could collaborate on a book together. I've known him since he was sixteen – I first interviewed him after he'd won the boys' singles at Wimbledon in 1998 – and the fact that I lived in Switzerland, speak German and French, and know several of the people with whom he grew up puts me in a unique position among international tennis writers to write his biography. Federer is a perfectionist, however, and after considering the idea he came back with the answer that, if he couldn't do something properly, he didn't want to do it at all. As he felt the time required to write an authorised biography or autobiography would be greater than he wanted to invest at this stage of his career, he politely declined. His mother Lynette told me, 'It's a nice problem to have when people want to write books about you, and we won't put any obstacles in your way, but Roger doesn't want to work on anything remotely official or authorised at this stage.'

Consequently, this is an unauthorised biography, and it draws on the recollections and memories of many of the people who shaped him in his childhood and early adulthood, and features quotes from interviews he has given over the years, plus a few comments from him elicited especially for this book. In addition, the Federer family have co-operated with me by supplying a number of photographs from the family album, in return for which John Blake Publishing has made a donation to the Roger Federer Foundation.

One day – probably shortly after Roger has hung up his racket for the last time – an official book about his life and career will appear, written with his direct collaboration. That's no doubt how it should be, because at twenty-four he probably has about sixty per cent of his playing career still ahead of him, so now is hardly the time for his self-penned memoirs. Instead here is a portrait of Roger Federer – the man, the player, the superstar who appears not to have been corrupted by fame and fortune. This is a book about a new arrival at the pinnacle of not just tennis but of sport in general.

I'm indebted to a number of people who have borne witness to Roger's development and have given me the benefit of their experience, including (in alphabetical order) Yves Allegro, Madeleine Bärlocher, Beat Caspar, Marco Chiudinelli, Roger Jaunin, Seppli Kacovski, Marco Mordasini, Francesco Ricci Bitti, Niki von Vary, Freddy Widmer and Thomas Wirz. I am also grateful for various bits of important help to Faye Andrews, Tim Curry, Richard Eaton, Tony Godsick, Mark Hodgkinson, Mitzi Ingram Evans, Annie Hammerton, Severin Lüthi, Ian McDermott, Konrad Meyer, Peter Miles, Jack Milner,

Helen Mittwoch, Daniel Monnin, Claudia Moser, Andrew Rigby, Neil Robinson, Barbara Travers and Paul Zimmer. I'd also like to thank Lynette Federer for her willingness to help. And, of course, thanks to John Blake and Michelle Signore of John Blake Publishing for having the belief in both me and the concept of this book to run with it.

Roger Federer is a remarkable sportsman and a remarkable person. If this book enables people to understand him better, it will have served its purpose.

Chris Bowers
April 2006

1

HAMBURG, MAY 2001. Roger Federer is playing the Argentinian Franco Squillari on an outside court at the Rothenbaum. Set amid the imposing architecture of the impressive Rothenbaumchaussee boulevard, it's a tennis venue that oozes prestige and tradition. It's also the venerable home of the Tennis Masters, Hamburg (the former German Open), one of the oldest tournaments in the world and one of the biggest outside the four Grand Slams. Yet the twenty-year-old Swiss prodigy delivers a patchy performance and, although he's the superior player in terms of natural talent, things aren't going well for him.

Squillari gets to match point. A rally ensues. Federer pushes the wily Argentinian left-hander back well behind his baseline and rushes to the net. It should be an easy volley. Squillari plays the ball with as much topspin as he can in an attempt to force Federer to play a low volley. His opponent loses sight of the ball and suddenly realises it's jammed between his racket and the heavy clay. In the background, the umpire calls, 'Game, set and match Squillari, 6–3, 6–4.'

Federer shakes Squillari's hand at the net, acknowledges the umpire and then smashes his racket in a rage under the umpire's chair.

This is not the kind of image most people associate with Federer, but of all the turning points – or significant stepping-stones – in his gradual rise to the top of his profession, this was perhaps the most significant. Here was a young man who, for half of his life, had thrown his racket when frustrated, sworn, wept, gone off into a sulk and generally given the impression that yet another gifted player might be about to squander his gifts by failing to have the right mental attitude to cope with the grind of the global tennis circuit.

His mother, Lynette, later recalled in a newspaper interview, 'I used to say to Roger, "When you have these outbursts like this, you're just telling your opponent that you're ready for him to beat you. You're sending out invitations. Is that what you want?"' And on another occasion, she said, 'This stage was part of his growing up, but, when his behaviour was bad, we told him it was bad and that it upset us. We used to say, "Come on, Roger. Get control of yourself. Pull yourself together. Is it such a catastrophe if you lose a match?"'

Federer himself admits, 'When I was ten, twelve,

fourteen, I was definitely at my worst. It was horrible, even funny sometimes – a lot of throwing rackets, making comments on every shot, because I just couldn't accept to lose. I was very talented and I thought, "How can it be that I'm not playing well?"'

At seventeen, he'd spent some time working with a psychologist, which had helped a little, but as he tried to make the transition from next-big-thing-waiting-to-happen to next-big-thing, the old problem of his wayward temper returned to haunt him. That smashed racket in Hamburg was perhaps one of the most valuable he has ever played with, because it made him take a long, hard look at himself. 'What made me upset was not just losing the match but my attitude,' he says today. 'I said there that I needed an attitude change. I remember thinking, "I never smash my racket after matches, only during matches." And then I said, "That's it. I'm not getting pissed off any more. I'm acting too bad."'

Although he says now that it took him a few months to get comfortable with his new attitude, the effect was instant. He went on to reach the quarter-finals at the French Open and then to end Pete Sampras's dominance of Wimbledon. In the space of eight weeks, Roger Federer had ended the reign of one tennis great and laid the most important foundation stone for his own.

2

ROGER FEDERER WAS born on 8 August 1981 in Switzerland's second-largest city, Basel, the second child and first son of Lynette and Robbie Federer, who had lived there since their marriage in 1973.

Though hardly a destination for the trendy international jetsetter, Basel's location on the Rhine river at the junction of three countries – Switzerland, Germany and France – makes it a highly appropriate place of origin for a global sporting icon. In fact, the city's location at an international crossroads had something of a role in Federer today being conversant in three languages – or four, if you consider the fiercely independent guttural Swiss-German dialects as a language in their own right. Five languages are regularly visible in everyday life in Basel: the four Swiss languages – German, French, Italian, the original pure Swiss language of Romansch (now spoken only in the east but still in use on banknotes and some official signs) and English. The city's airport, sited on French territory, was for years known as Basel–Mulhouse but is today known as Euro-Airport, which cities in Germany, Switzerland and France all claim as their own.

As the most European city in a country whose inhabitants are still very sceptical about joining the European Union, Basel has a mildly un-Swiss character and a sense of humour all of its own. It has its own variation of the German carnival called the *Morgestraich* (literally, 'morning roam through the streets'), a pagan procession held on the Monday after Ash Wednesday at 4am, at which time all the lights in the city go off to enhance the effect of a stream of candlelit torches. It's also one of Europe's oldest university cities and a centre of the European pharmaceuticals industry. (It was in Basel in 1943 that a chemist, Professor Albert Hofmann, tested on himself a molecule he had devised and named LSD-25 – when he began having hallucinations, it became clear he had become the first man to experience the effects of the drug commonly known today as LSD.)

Roger Federer's story begins in the Basel pharmaceuticals industry, though somewhat less prosaically. His father, Robert, was a laboratory assistant with the Basel-based chemicals giant Ciba-Geigy. As the 1960s ended, he was posted to Ciba's main plant in South Africa, which was based in Isando, an industrial suburb on the east rand of Johannesburg. There in 1970 he met an 18-year-old secretary, Lynette Durand, who worked at Ciba and had lived all her life in the affluent nearby suburb of Kempton Park. They soon discovered they had a shared interest in tennis, got to know each other better outside work, and began a romance, which led to marriage in 1973.

Robbie Federer was born in 1946. He grew up in eastern Switzerland near the town of Altstätten, and played tennis for fun, but never aspired to doing it particularly well. Lynette is six years his junior, born in 1952 to a family whose first language was Afrikaans. She played tennis to a much higher level than her husband – according to Beat Caspar, the sports editor of Basel's daily newspaper, the *Basler Zeitung*, 'She had a good sense of co-ordination, much better than Robert' – but, despite having a fair amount of ambition, she too never aspired to make a career of it.

In 1973, the couple moved to Switzerland – leaving Lynette 8,400 kilometres (5,200 miles) from 'home' – and settled in Riehen, a suburb of Basel near the German border. (The English-speaking world is still not entirely sure how it wants to spell and pronounce Switzerland's second city. 'Basel', pronounced *Barsl*, is the Swiss German name and, as it is a Swiss German city, that is the local name. It's also the spelling and pronunciation used on the tennis circuit for the Swiss Indoors tournament that takes place there every October. But there is an old English version 'Basle', pronounced *Barl*, derived from the city's French name 'Bâle', pronounced as in the English word *balcony*, which dates from the days when most major European cities had an English spelling and is still used by some British newspapers. This book uses the local spelling of 'Basel'.)

Robert went on to become a sales executive for Ciba while Lynette also secured a posting with the company in her new home city, and the two played tennis at the firm's multi-sports club, which had a handful of courts shaded by mature trees. Company sports and leisure grounds were a very cheap way for employees to practise their recreation, in fact some companies allowed their staff and their families to use the firm's facilities for free. That was fine for the bank balance but often led to an atmosphere in which the more ambitious social players became frustrated.

After a few years at Basel, Lynette joined the 'Old Boys' Tennis Club, one of Basel's top two tennis clubs (the other being the equally Swiss-sounding 'Basel Lawn Tennis Club'), mainly to play competitive matches, and on three occasions she was a member of the Old Boys' women's team that became Swiss national inter-club champions in the 'Young Veterans' age group. She also actively supported local and regional tennis, serving on the board of the Basel regional subsection of the Swiss Tennis Association and taking on responsibility for developing young natural talent. For many years, she also staffed the Old Boys' stand at Basel's ATP tournament, the Swiss Indoors. Today she plays virtually no tennis, instead preferring golf, at which she currently boasts a handicap of around fifteen.

The remarkable thing is that both Robbie and Lynette were very short. Neither is more than 1.7m (5ft 7in), and for a while it was feared that any offspring of theirs couldn't possibly grow tall enough to become a force on the tennis circuit. Yet, out of some genetic inheritance, Roger Federer has grown to 1.85m (6ft 1in).

In late 1979, Lynette and Robbie's first child, Diana, was born. A much quieter person than her younger brother, she has quite deliberately kept out of the limelight, and has pursued her own career as a psychiatric nurse, working outside but not far from Basel.

The Federers appear to have largely avoided the classic trap of having a gifted child whose interest needs to be serviced to such an extent that other offspring suffer. 'The family was always relatively harmonious,' says Thomas Wirz, a Basel journalist and tennis coach who on several occasions carried out interviews in the Federer family home. 'I have sometimes wondered what Diana did while Roger was being ferried from tournament to tournament, and she may well have certain misgivings about the tennis world, but she has always seemed very independent, pretty sure of herself and very polite. There certainly never seemed to be any sense of resentment.'

Diana, who enjoys skiing and snowboarding, was often approached by the *Basler Zeitung* for quotes. 'She never wanted to have an article about herself in the newspaper,' says Beat Caspar. 'I often asked her. I told her the people would be interested in her, especially when they see her sitting courtside watching Roger's matches, but she always said no. Lynette constantly made it clear that Diana wasn't to get the short straw from Roger's tennis. She always told

Diana that she shouldn't be in any way bothered by the fact that people were always asking about Roger. And Diana has always kept her distance from tennis and the media, and has never wanted to talk publicly about her brother.'

Twenty months after Diana's birth, after the family had moved across the Rhine to Münchenstein, a suburb closer to Basel city centre, Roger was born. With no middle name, the birth register simply bears the entry: 'Roger Federer'. Because he's Swiss, and because French is the second language in Switzerland, many assume that his first name is pronounced the French way (eg as in *Roget's Thesaurus*), but, as he has often had to point out, it is pronounced the English way, and most French-speaking people who know this have developed their own pronunciation (as if written 'Roj-air'). The correct pronunciation of 'Federer' has the emphasis on the first syllable, with the vowel sound somewhere between the vowel in the English words 'fair' and 'fay' and the first 'r' flipped. The English-speaking world has settled into a pronunciation that resembles the English word 'federal', a pronunciation that Federer accepts as legitimate.

What was he like as a boy? In an interview in 2005, Lynette said, 'He wasn't a straightforward child. He was very, very lively, full of energy, and he was always trying out the boundaries with his parents – and, later, with his teachers – in sport, in school. He was always a bundle of energy and very emotional, not easy to be with. For a while, I was constantly worried about his concentration, but he later worked on that.'

The Swiss education system offers each Swiss canton (administrative district) a fair bit of freedom in its educational set-up. In Basel, then as now, children went to kindergarten at five, primary school at seven, secondary school at eleven or twelve and then on to various forms of further education at fifteen or sixteen, once the compulsory years were over.

Roger followed his sister Diana into the Neuewelt School, a state-run primary school in a quiet leafy and affluent corner of Münchenstein – the name 'Neuewelt' literally means 'new world' but it is just the name of an area in Münchenstein and doesn't indicate any wider idealistic project. Although they could have afforded to send their children to private schools, Robbie and Lynette's decision to send Diana and Roger to the local state primary wasn't unusual, as that was very much what one did in Switzerland. There was little demand for private schools, especially in moderately well-off areas where facilities were good, and it was felt that parental support encouraged high standards of education. The Neuewelt School had both a kindergarten and a primary school, and both Diana and Roger went there from five to twelve.

Data-protection legislation and other privacy safeguards prevent Roger's teachers from saying too much about his schooling, but Theresa Fischbacher, who was head teacher for part of the time Roger was in his primary-school years, remembers him more from his time outside the classroom than in it. 'I was convinced he would become a footballer,' she recalls. 'You hardly ever saw him without a football at his feet, and he used to say, "I want to become a footballer!" For a long time, I had no idea he played tennis and, when I eventually found out, I assumed it had to be very much a secondary activity because of his passion for football. I have to admit that he was very good, and it wouldn't have surprised me to see him make it as a football player.'

A few years before Roger arrived at the Neuewelt School, two of its alumni, the brothers Murat and Hakan Yakin, had been as enthusiastic footballers in their primary-school days as Federer and went on to become local icons for FC Basel, each playing more than forty games for the Swiss national team. Their success created a culture at the school that it was cool to play football, and, with tennis at that time still a very limited sport in a country whose primary sporting passions were football, skiing and ice hockey, young Roger might well have felt more comfortable with the big ball at his feet than the small ball on his racket strings.

Fischbacher remembers one other thing about him: 'He was always moving. He was happy, had a lovely nature and was well brought up, in terms of his manners, but he had this constant need to be on the move. He was a fidget.' Yet she denies that this restlessness in any way made him a bad pupil. 'He was clearly bright, and I've known many restless, fidgety kids who were very bright.'

Federer himself says of his primary-school days, 'I loved playing with balls, whatever sport they were from: ping-pong, tennis, basketball, football. I was always trying something.'

At twelve, he left to attend the Progymnasium, a form of secondary school specifically for children expected to go on to the full Gymnasium (literally 'grammar school', although not really comparable to the English grammar schools) at the age of fifteen. Although he never went on to the full Gymnasium, never excelled in academic pursuits and finished his schooling at Switzerland's National Tennis Centre, he wouldn't have been allowed into the Progymnasium if he hadn't been at least moderately bright.

One might expect there to be pictures of such inspirational alumni as the Yakin brothers and Roger Federer adorning the corridors of the Neuewelt School. In some countries, there might even have been a plaque, 'ROGER FEDERER WENT TO SCHOOL HERE, 1988–93'. But no. Switzerland just isn't that sort of country. For today's pupils, parents and staff at the school, Federer is just someone who went there a couple of decades ago. Perhaps this lack of ostentatious admiration provides one part-explanation for Federer's phenomenal normality and humanity in the face of the global admiration he enjoys today.

The Federers often holidayed in South Africa, but these trips largely dried up when both Roger and Diana were at school. In an interview with the South African *Sunday Times*, Lynette recalled, 'When the children were still young we used to come to South Africa more often, but when they went to school we couldn't return as often because the European summer holidays are in South Africa's winter, which isn't so appealing. But my kids love South Africa very, very much, especially the Garden Route [a popular tourist stretch of the south coast of South Africa between Cape Town and Port Elizabeth]. When Roger was still in his teens, we spent a holiday on the south coast. He loves the game and the wildlife.'

One of the bibles of the global tennis circuit is what used to be known as the annual Media Guide, now re-termed *The Official Guide to Professional Tennis*, brought out by the ATP (originally the Association of Tennis Professionals) and the WTA Tour (originally Women's Tennis Association). It's a guide to the global tennis circus, but the meat of it is the biographies of leading tennis players, including their results, vital statistics, general career summary and a few personal details. Each of the seven editions of the guide in which Federer has featured (since 2000) has recorded that he started to play tennis at the age of eight, a figure out by five years – it's mildly astonishing that someone hasn't thought to tell the ATP that its normally reliable guide has such an oft-repeated error. It's true that he didn't start to take tennis seriously until he was eight, but he first picked up a racket not long after his third birthday. There's even a picture of him holding a wooden racket by the throat (it being too heavy for a three-year-old to wield by holding the grip), taken at the Ciba Club, his father's works club, in late 1984. Roger's story is like that of many players who go on to make it as professionals: his parents played as a hobby and at weekends took him along to their club, where he picked up a racket and was soon hooked. 'He loved the sport from the beginning,' his mother has said.

When he wasn't seeking out youngsters at the Ciba Club to mess around with, Federer would take his racket and hit ball after ball against the garage door of the family home. 'I remember always loving to play against the garage door,' he said in an interview in 2005, 'or even against the cupboard doors inside, with any kind of ball. My mum got fed up because it was bang, bang, bang, all day.'

He was taken to a handful of tennis clinics, and at the age of six or seven he attended a training course organised in the Basel suburb of Allschwil by the VBTU, the regional association of tennis clubs in greater Basel. The course involved a dozen under-tens receiving coaching on three full-length courts. It was there he met Marco Chiudinelli, a boy just thirty-three days his junior, who went on to become one of his best friends and who would one day deputise for him in the Swiss Davis Cup team.

By the time his eighth birthday came around, Federer was still playing at the Ciba Club. He had no rating, so by default was R9 (the lowest category in the system by which players are classified in Switzerland). His mother continued to play to a higher level at the TC Old Boys, but she was becoming aware of her son's talent, and also that her club had a framework in which Roger could prosper, one more suited to him than the Ciba Club's. One day, she approached Madeleine Bärlocher, who had taken over the dilapidated Old Boys' junior programme in 1980 and put some new life into it, and said, 'I have a son who plays tennis to a good level. You have a good junior programme. I would like you to take my son into your junior set-up.'

With that, Roger Federer became the new boy at Old Boys, and took the step that brought him into contact with the people who taught him how to play tennis.

3

THE TENNIS ENVIRONMENT into which Roger Federer was thrust at the age of eight was ready-made for a promising young talent. Madeleine Bärlocher, a secretary who had played in the Wimbledon juniors in 1959 in the days long before tennis was ever likely to offer career prospects, had a recipe that was hardly revolutionary – she just set in train fixed squads with a regime of private one-to-one coaching and group training, all at fixed times every week, some of it funded by money from youth sports foundations. And it worked. She brought in appropriate coaches and within a short time had vindicated her belief that, if you can attract one or two good people, a lot more good people will follow.

Although set in the affluent leafy suburbs of Binningen to the west of Basel city centre, the TC Old Boys was hardly a magnet for the rich. Founded in 1927, it was –

and is – an outdoor club with just seven clay courts and a modest clapperboard clubhouse. The only indoor facilities it has to this day are two courts covered by an inflatable bubble. If members want to play indoors during the winter months, they generally have to rely on the club's arrangement with the *Paradies* indoor tennis centre, owned by Roger Brennwald, the Basel sports impresario who owns and runs the Swiss Indoors ATP tournament every October in the city's premier indoor arena, the St Jakobshalle.

In the 1980s, tennis was still very much a fringe sport in Switzerland. The country's main passions were football and winter sports. Advertising hoardings featuring sports stars were largely the preserve of Pirmin Zurbriggen, Maria Walliser and Vreni Schneider, a photogenic trio who headed a golden age in Swiss skiing, which itself followed on the heels of an earlier golden age headed by Bernhard Russi and Erika Hess.

In 1987, the tennis fraternity was boosted when Switzerland finally qualified for the Davis Cup world group with a team featuring Jakob Hlasek, Claudio Mezzadri and the veteran doubles specialist Heinz Günthardt, who had won a Wimbledon doubles title in 1985. The Swiss chose to play their first world group tie in Basel in the St Jakobshalle, losing in February 1988 to the French team of Yannick Noah, Henri Leconte and Guy Forget. Hlasek had broken his wrist in a car accident a couple of months earlier and couldn't play, but he came back to post his best year on the tour, finishing in the top ten and finally putting Switzerland on the map as a tennis-playing nation.

In the mid-1990s, Old Boys had a promising player in Emmanuel Marmillod, a naturally gifted left-hander who might have blazed a trail for Federer to follow, but it was not to be. There are those who believe Marmillod was also partly undone by a general lack of ambition in Swiss tennis. 'When a promising player came along,' recalls Bärlocher, 'we tended to think of them as being potentially nationally ranked but never really world ranked. That was also the case when Roger arrived: we just didn't think in big terms because we had never had anyone who had reached those heights.'

Old Boys' connection with world tennis came via two channels: the annual Swiss Indoors tournament at Basel's St Jakobshalle and the presence of a few professionals in the Swiss national inter-club league. There was a tradition of each of the top league clubs enlisting the services of one touring professional – usually in the twilight of his or her career – to come and play a few matches a year in the summer months. This arrangement gave the clubs the chance to make their team more attractive and increase their chances of winning, and they were prevented from paying the players anything more than their expenses (at least officially).

Old Boys had a national A-League team, and in the late 1970s they recruited the British player John Feaver, who reached ninety-eighth in the world rankings back in 1973, to play three seasons between 1979 and 1981. Feaver was so enamoured of the camaraderie and opportunities presented by inter-club leagues such as Switzerland's that he started a national league in Britain. 'The reasons we played were that you could get good, competitive clay-court matches,' he recalls. 'That was particularly attractive for the British players, as there were limited clay courts and no inter-club in the UK – and it was also really good fun. You had a nice evening after the match – a steak, a few beers. Sometimes they'd even ring the church bells. For some matches, we had a couple of hundred spectators, especially when you had teams each with a touring professional, so the singles match in which the two number ones played each other could be quite attractive. It was a great breeding ground for young players to get some good experience.'

Another touring pro who landed in Basel was Peter Carter, a shy Australian in his mid-twenties. And perhaps the single most beneficial thing Bärlocher did for Federer was to persuade Carter to do some junior-squad coaching.

Carter was a touring professional from the Barossa Valley, north of Adelaide, who reached 173rd in the ATP rankings in the 1980s. He was coached in his teens by Peter Smith, an Australian who played a part in the formative years of many Australian tennis players, including John Fitzgerald, Darren Cahill, Broderick Dyke and Lleyton Hewitt. Cahill and Carter were the same age, and Smith later said Carter was arguably the better of the two. But, by 1989, Carter was approaching twenty-five, dogged by injury and sliding down the rankings, so he accepted an offer to play a year's league tennis for Old Boys in the Swiss national A-League. He proved a hit there and enjoyed the experience, so he stayed for another year.

That second year, Madeleine Bärlocher asked him if he was willing to take a junior-squad coaching session. Carter was taken aback and had to fight off his initial instinct to say no. After giving the matter some thought, he agreed to try it. Despite having very little German, he found a way of communicating easily with the juniors, proved a natural at coaching and settled into a role looking after the club's squads that was to last until 1997. 'He had a sunny boy image,' recalls the Basel journalist and tennis coach Thomas Wirz about Carter, 'but underneath he was very serious. That combination really works for Roger. And he also played a very similar style to Roger: very classical strokes, especially the one-handed backhand.'

So when, in 1989, the eight-year-old Roger Federer arrived at Old Boys, he found not only a structure in place to meet all his needs but also an understated but highly disciplined character from the English-speaking southern hemisphere to guide him through squad training. Even though they didn't work together for a year or so, Federer had met one of the people who was to shape his career most profoundly. One night, a couple of years later, the Australian phoned home and told his dad, 'Oh, have I got a young boy here who looks promising. He's only about twelve or thirteen, but I think he's going to go places.'

But Federer also needed someone who could teach him to play tennis. He'd clearly demonstrated an aptitude for the sport at the Ciba Club and against his garage wall, but he needed someone to hone his strokes, to teach him footwork and general movement, and to give him the weapons that would one day conquer the world. That man was Seppli Kacovski.

Adolf Kacovski – 'Seppli' is a nickname he picked up in Switzerland – is a Czech who had the good fortune to be coaching in Tunisia when Soviet tanks rolled into Prague in August 1968 to crush what was known as the 'Prague Spring'. Once Alexander Dubcek, the Czechoslovak leader who had tried to practise what he called 'communism with a human face', had been deposed, it was virtually impossible for Czechoslovak citizens to travel abroad, a situation that lasted until the Velvet Revolution of 1989 swept away Soviet-controlled rule. Had he been at home, Kacovski might never have escaped the country and the Roger Federer story would have been somewhat different. But in 1969, Kacovski – by then an asylum seeker – was enticed to Basel to become the principal coach at the Old Boys club and given the priority of 'furthering the juniors and young talent in general'.

Kacovski, whose motto translates as 'we're going further', introduced a number of features to Old Boys. His main innovation was the introduction a 'godfather' system of having a more experienced player assigned to youngsters as sparring partner and mentor. He also brought with him a strong sense of ambition.

When Federer arrived at Old Boys in 1989, it was Kacovski's job to give him one-to-one coaching. Of all the people who knew Federer there, Kacovski is the only one who claims to have seen the boy's potential from the start. 'When he came to me, after one or two days I knew this was a massive talent,' he recalls. 'I've been a tennis coach for more than forty years, and after that time you know who's got talent and who hasn't. After two days, I knew Roger was born with a racket in his hand. Everything about him suggested his talent: his speed off the mark, his footwork, his willingness to work hard – everything.'

Kacovski also recognised something else about Federer with which he personally identified: the fact that he was only half Swiss. 'I come from the East,' he says, 'and I have a very different attitude to sport. I'm much more ambitious, and at one stage I had to tone down my coaching because the Swiss weren't happy. Some of them complained that I was too ambitious for them. I believe Roger is more ambitious because he isn't one hundred per cent Swiss. His father is very Swiss, and the calmness that Roger has comes from his father, but the ambition and willpower come from his mother, who's not Swiss.'

Kacovski's theory is supported by others, including Niki von Vary, a teammate of Federer's in the 1990s and now president of the Old Boys club. 'Here in Switzerland, sport isn't as accepted as it is in many other countries as a profession to go into,' he says. 'We're pretty keen on the security of a learned apprenticeship, and in that context sport is viewed somewhat suspiciously as a way to make your living.'

And Köbi Kuhn, the highly regarded coach of the Swiss

national football team, has said his job has been made easier by the influx of Swiss players with dual nationality, especially those whose second nationality is from countries – many from south-eastern Europe – where football has a much higher priority than it does in Switzerland. He says it has made more of his team keener to succeed than the all-Swiss national teams Kuhn himself was part of in his playing days.

For six years – from the ages of eight to fourteen – Seppli Kacovski and Peter Carter were Roger Federer's coaches. Kacovski, an ardent fan of the one-handed backhand, did the one-to-one work, Carter looked after squad coaching and refined some elements of Federer's game, and Madeleine Bärlocher ran the Old Boys' junior team for inter-club matches. Roger also had input from two other coaches, Haiggi Abt and Daniel Gerber, through the squads run by the VBTU, the regional association of tennis clubs in greater Basel, one of a dozen regional subsections of the national tennis association. It was a perfect environment for a talented, quick-to-learn and ambitious young tennis player.

But such ambition was not always his own. Bärlocher recalls an early practice session in which the young Roger wanted to play with his friends, even if they weren't the best players. 'His mother asked me to put him with the best,' she says, 'so I did, but his friends weren't the best, so Roger came to me and said, "I told you I wanted to play with my friends." He didn't have any fear of playing against the best, but it was more important to him to play with the people he liked. But his mother insisted I put him with the best, and that's where he ended up.'

Federer is sometimes asked by fan magazines and other publications who his idols were when he was growing up. The name he gives most often is Boris Becker, but Stefan Edberg and Pete Sampras also crop up. He admits that the fact that all three play with one-handed backhands was part of the attraction – although Federer always played his backhand the traditional way, Edberg and Sampras learned with two hands and switched to the one-hander in their teens. And Federer also stresses that admiration for a given player did not make him want to copy them – his playing style is his own.

Many of those who remember Federer from that time describe him as a *Lausbub*, a Swiss-German word that best translates as a fun-loving rascal or rogue. There is certainly nothing malicious meant, and he clearly had a strong sense of fun. On one occasion, for example, at a team match at another Basel club, there weren't enough courts for everyone to play concurrently, so Federer had to wait his turn. Then, when a court finally became free, no one could find him – he had climbed a tree overlooking the club to observe what was going on, and to see how long it would take for people to find him.

Much of his sense of fun came as part of a double act with his friend Marco Chiudinelli, who proved something of a late developer and reached 129th in the world rankings in early 2005 before a shoulder injury took him back to square one. Both boys lived in the Basel suburb of

Münchenstein, the Federers in Im Wasserhaus, the Chiudinellis 200m around the corner in Poppelweg, and they frequently met up on their bikes and cycled to Old Boys, where they practised together before cycling home together again. 'We played a lot of sports,' recalls Chiudinelli. 'We were always pretty much on the same level, except for tennis which he always won. We also used to play squash together on the squash court with tennis rackets and a squash ball. It was pretty dangerous – certainly for the rackets!'

Another person who uses the term *Lausbub* to describe Federer is Niki von Vary, who says, 'It was never boring with him around. He and Marco Chiudinelli were best friends – they're the same age and grew up with us at the club – and when those two were together, then we knew the crazy gang was around and the calm of the tennis club disappeared.'

Practice sessions were particularly difficult. 'We used to mess around in practice,' says Chiudinelli. 'We lost interest very quickly and used to talk a lot. There was a lot of unrest. Rackets used to fly around in all directions, which was probably the most dangerous thing that happened. We were frequently sent on training runs or just sent home. Peter Carter didn't have an easy time with us.'

While Marco and Roger engaged in typical boys' posturing, Bärlocher picked up on something that proved to be prophetic: 'Whenever Roger was messing around with his friends, he'd always say, "I'm going to be number one." He'd hit a great smash, and then he'd stop and say, "That's the shot I'm going to win Wimbledon with."

It was obviously a joke – all boys do that – but that's what he used to say.'

The less agreeable side to the fun-loving personality was his temper, a far cry from the calm and composed figure Federer cuts on court today. One of his coaches even referred to him as 'a little Satan' on court. He would throw his racket, scream and swear, and had great difficulty accepting defeat.

There was one notorious match when Federer was eleven. Whenever he played locally, he always seemed to come up against Danny Schnyder, the younger brother of Patty Schnyder, who went on to be ranked in the women's top ten. Danny was Roger's first nemesis. One year, the two played in the final of the Basel Junior Championships, Schnyder the Swiss number one and Federer the Swiss number two in the under-twelves age group. Thomas Wirz recalls, 'They played that match and threw their rackets and swore, and both of them got a warning from the supervisor. It was horrific, but also quite amusing.'

Madeleine Bärlocher says Federer could never stand it when an opponent played a really nice point against him. 'He'd often say, "Lucky!", and a couple of times I had to say to him, "Hang on. There are others who can play good tennis as well, you know." The fact is that he never liked to lose, and you see that today in his attitude towards players who have regularly beaten him, like Agassi, Hewitt and Nalbandian.'

On one occasion after a defeat in an inter-club match, he was so angry that he cried his eyes out and hid under the umpire's chair, whereupon Bärlocher, his team supervisor, had a hard time persuading him to come out. Years later, she asked Federer if he remembered that scene. Federer said no. But he did remember another incident that also gives an insight into the youngster's character.

In one of his first Basel League inter-club matches, Old Boys were playing away at a club with only two courts and not a great reputation. At ten, Federer was the youngest and the smallest in the six-member team, and with a format of six singles and three doubles there was a lot of waiting around for matches to finish and courts to become free. Federer wasn't in one of the first two matches to go on court, and during the first matches it became clear that there was one player from the other team who kept screaming from the side, trying to influence line calls. Bärlocher intervened and some angry words were exchanged. Aware of the bad blood developing between the teams, she decided not to play Federer in the singles. 'He was the youngest, he would have been up against someone who wasn't playing fair on line calls, and I was worried that something would happen,' she recounts. 'And he was so angry with me because I wouldn't let him play singles, only doubles. He remembers that! I was concerned that they'd look at him and say, "Oh, that little kid. We can have some fun with him. We can call lines our way and he won't stand up to us." I knew that Roger was very fixated on the truth. He had a very powerful sense of fairness. He never took a call for himself that he felt wasn't absolutely right but, if someone on the other side of the net made a call that Roger knew was wrong, he'd be so angry that he'd start throwing his racket. That's why I didn't want to risk him. I wanted to protect him, but he was mad with me.'

Tears of frustration and ambition were a regular feature of Federer's junior matches, but he also had a charitable side to his nature. Marco Chiudinelli tells a story from the first time he played Federer in an official match. 'We were about eight or nine. He wasn't very good at losing, and I wasn't either. After about six games he'd opened up a considerable lead and I began to cry, so he came up to me at the change of ends and started consoling me, said, "It'll get better" – and it did. About five games later, I'd taken the lead, and then he began to cry, so I went up to him and said, "Take it easy," and he came back to win. In retrospect, it was a beautiful moment, because you can see that we were friends.'

Federer has admitted that there were times when he would be aware of his parents watching him from the Old Boys' terrace while he was losing his temper on court. Occasionally, they would call out for him to be quiet, and on one such occasion he shot back, 'Go and have a drink and leave me alone.' Federer said that the family would then drive home 'in a quiet car with no one speaking; I would carry on like an idiot.'

In general, the tightly wound bundle of emotion on the court was very polite and well mannered off it. Local journalists who dealt with him at that time speak of a happy and helpful boy, and Federer clearly recognised convincing authority figures when he saw them. Bärlocher says he seldom threw his racket when she was in charge, although his language could be colourful, which caused concern with his parents. 'I once had Lynette coming up to me, asking me to say something about his cursing,' she recalls, 'but I thought it was pretty harmless, and he always behaved pretty well with me. I had a lot of kids who behaved a lot worse than Roger. I was keen to enforce good standards of behaviour because I knew that anything bad [would reflect poorly] on the club.'

Seppli Kacovski noticed something else about Federer's on-court tantrums. 'I've known enough players who play a bad match,' he says. 'They scream at themselves, can't accept a defeat and say, "I'm giving up. I'm not playing tennis any more." Roger never said that. He got angry, he had difficulty accepting defeats, but he never once said, "I'm giving up."'

When Federer beat Gaston Gaudio 6–0, 6–0 in the semi-finals of the 2005 Tennis Masters Cup in Shanghai, he was asked whether it was true that he'd never until then won a match with that score. 'Yes, it is,' he said, before adding, 'I have lost one 6–0, 6–0, but that was in juniors.'

It was actually his first match of any consequence. At the age of ten, he was picked to play in a junior tournament for children under twelve. (The age rules mean you can play in the under-twelves when you're twelve, as long as you were still eleven at the start of the year.) In the first round, Federer came up against a twelve-year-old called Reto Schmidli – at that age, two years can make a major difference and, with Federer one of the smaller boys in his year at that stage, it did. He didn't win a single game. Asked about the defeat many years later, he replied, 'It's the only 6–0, 6–0 loss I've ever had, and I didn't play that badly!'

Today, Schmidli still lives in the Basel area and occasionally runs into Federer. When he does, Roger always reminds him that he was the only player ever to beat him 6–0, 6–0 – not a bad claim to fame, given the heights Federer has scaled as a professional.

At eleven, Federer was ranked number two in his age group in Switzerland, and on 13 July 1992 he made his first few column centimetres in the local daily, the *Basler Zeitung*. He had lost in the final of a national under-twelves event for lower-rated players to the Geneva-based Japanese player Jun Kato, who later went on to play one Davis Cup match for Japan. A year later, however, Federer won the Swiss under-twelves national championship. But could anyone at that stage truly have said that this was a champion in the making?

To their credit, most people who remember him say no. 'There are plenty of people who like to think they saw it coming,' says Niki von Vary, 'but, as far as I can remember, no one ever seriously expected Roger to go as far as he's gone. Certainly not when he was eleven or twelve.'

Thomas Wirz remembers watching the twelve-year-old Federer at the time he won the national under-twelves championship, but he also remembers thinking the youngster's on-court temper tantrums might hold him back.

'You could see very early what good hands he had, but he'd play two or three good points and then do something wild, and he often threw his racket. He wasn't that disciplined, so it's hard to say that he was headed for greatness.'

Even in 1992, the year Marc Rosset won the gold medal for Switzerland at the Barcelona Summer Olympics and he and Jakob Hlasek steered the Swiss to their first Davis Cup final, there was still a lack of ambition in the Swiss ranks. 'At that time the Swiss level wasn't that high, so we didn't look that high,' says Madeleine Bärlocher. 'As a result, I can't say I or any of us ever thought Roger would go as far as he has. I always said to him, "Rogi, whatever it is you want to achieve in tennis, you have to decide for yourself. We can help you, but in principle you have to know what you want to achieve." We had a lot of good juniors, and he was always the youngest, so we knew he was good, but potentially world number one? I'd have to say no.'

What about those who knew him on court? 'I thought he'd make it on to the tour,' says Marco Chiudinelli, 'because from an early age he saw off his Swiss competition and did seem to have something special, but I don't think anyone at that time could have suggested he'd achieve what he's done.'

The only member of the Basel contingent in direct contact with Federer in the early 1990s who claims to have seen the potential for greatness is Seppli Kacovski, the man who taught him his strokes. Kacovski is a strict yet immensely likeable sexagenarian who oozes an enthusiasm for tennis that he manages to communicate to the youngsters he coaches today. It's easy to imagine him getting excited about the fluent strokes of a youngster, but he says it was Federer's ability to learn and bounce back from defeats that gave him such hope for the lad. 'The learning process went so quickly with him, and I never had to repeat anything. He had an enormous ability to grasp what I was telling him. I always say it's a long cable between the head and the racket to describe how long it takes most people to grasp what I'm coaching them, but Roger just got it straight away. I saw it; the coaches saw it; the club saw it.'

Kacovski also noticed that Federer's willingness to learn matched his ability to learn. 'Even back then he hated losing, but he had the ability to draw the conclusion that, "If I don't want to lose, I have to put in the work." If he won 6–1, 6–1, he'd often wonder how he could have won 6–0, 6–0. I was pretty hard with him, though in a friendly way. He was quite small – certainly smaller and physically less robust than everyone else – but then he played with such great technique, and that allowed him to win a lot of matches where he was physically inferior. But then, his father isn't tall, so we weren't sure how tall he'd end up.

'And he never had enough coaching,' Kacovski adds. 'We'd have a long coaching session, he'd work very hard, and then, when it was all over, he'd go to hit against the wall or seek out a sparring partner to hit some more. And he always used to say, "I'm going to be number one!" No one believed him. We could see that he had the potential to be a big star in Swiss tennis, but he was saying he was going to be *world* number one. He's not the only thirteen- or fourteen-year-old to have said that, but he had it in his head, and he worked towards achieving it.'

All of which may be true, but the *Basler Zeitung*'s sports editor, Beat Caspar, remembers Kacovski having problems with Federer at the beginning. 'He might well have recognised his talent, but he also had to remove Federer from training sessions because Federer was, at times, impossible. For a long time he wasn't allowed to practise with the best because his head was always stuffed full of silly ideas.'

But there was a distraction: football. Federer's love of all sports, especially ball games, had made him a highly proficient footballer. He joined the club Concordia Basel and played as a striker. 'I'm personally convinced that, if he'd chosen football, he'd have made it to the Swiss national team,' recalls Seppli Kacovski. 'I only saw him twice, but he scored three goals in those two matches, and in one of them he took the ball in his own half, dribbled 60m with it and scored. He just had it.'

Federer admits today that he thought he was 'pretty good, pretty skilful' at football, and he played the game with the same passion and competitiveness that he gave to tennis. His friend Marco Chiudinelli also played, having joined the FC Basel youth team, and on a few occasions the two came up against each other. 'We were both so determined to win,' Marco says. 'When we won, he cried. And when Concordia won, I cried. It meant a lot to us.'

Part of the Federer folklore is the claim that he was offered junior terms with FC Basel. This is almost certainly a myth, and he himself denies ever having received such an offer. Although it's true that today football clubs are showing an increasing interest in pre-teenage talent, in the early 1990s FC Basel had its own youth team, and Federer played for another club. (When asked about it now, Federer says, 'I wish I had had an offer!') Since he's become famous as a tennis player, there have been offers for him to train with the FC Basel squad, but, while he's been happy to be photographed with the club's players, he has always turned down any chance to train with them, no doubt through fear of suffering an injury that could harm his tennis.

Once he'd become national under-twelves champion in tennis, the question of which sport he should concentrate on became increasingly urgent. 'I was practising tennis and soccer in the week,' he says, 'but I was tending to favour tennis over soccer, so I couldn't attend all the soccer practice sessions. The coach eventually told me that if I didn't attend all the sessions he couldn't really put me in the team for matches at the weekend. And I couldn't make all the matches anyway because I was also trying to play tennis tournaments, even though I felt I was in one of the best soccer teams and playing in an age group above my own age. But I knew that I couldn't do both soccer and tennis until I die, that I would have had to improve my left foot – which was never a strength of mine back then – so I eventually made the decision to go for tennis.'

The fact that his parents were both into tennis – his mother seriously so – probably helped sway the decision and, although he occasionally wonders what would have happened had he opted for football, it's not a decision he's ever regretted. 'I like tennis more, and I like to be in control. In tennis, it's up to me – I can't blame defeats on goalies or something like that. So I'm happy I chose tennis. In the end, it wasn't a difficult decision.'

Having honed the strokes that Seppli Kacovski taught him, Federer by twelve was finding it was Peter Carter who was having a growing influence on his game. Although Carter was never Federer's personal coach at Old Boys (his main role was that of group trainer), his growing assurance as a coach brought on the games of many of those in his squads. 'If you had to define the attribute of calmness in a person, in whatever context, then Peter Carter was your perfect example,' says the Swiss journalist Marco Mordasini. 'He formed [Roger]. He took this bundle of energy, took the components and put them together, almost like taking a rough diamond and polishing it up.'

And Madeleine Bärlocher, who had brought Carter into the Old Boys' squad-coaching set-up, remembers, 'The training with Peter Carter was optimal, both in tennis terms and on a human level. Peter was very personable but very restrained; he never pushed himself into the foreground. If a youngster had problems, he'd always take them aside and talk with them. He could talk very well with the juniors, but, if someone behaved badly, he threw them out. Sometimes he sent Roger home.'

Marco Chiudinelli feels Carter had the great attribute of being able to tell each of his charges what they needed to do to improve. 'It was a great time with Peter Carter,' he says. 'There are three periods in my career when I was really able to raise my level, and the first of them was when I came to Old Boys and worked with Peter. I think Roger had the same thing, because, while Seppli was a very good teacher, Roger needed Peter to take him to the next level.'

There was still the unresolved issue of Federer's on-court outbursts. He would frequently go out on court, settle into a nice rhythm and then start having fun and lose his concentration. Some people at Old Boys were concerned that he might squander his talent in a whirl of joking around and losing his cool, but Carter helped him to keep moving forwards in his game.

Federer had one other bit of exposure to top-level tennis: as a ballboy. For a couple of years in the mid-1990s, he and Marco Chiudinelli were ballboys at the Swiss Indoors ATP event, which gave them the opportunity to rub shoulders with some of the biggest names in the sport. They were also asked to ballboy at Old Boys for a women's satellite tournament the club staged every year until 2002. That was 1994, when the two finalists were Martina Hingis and Patty Schnyder, who along with Federer himself went on to become three of the five most successful Swiss tennis players ever.

By the spring of 1995, Federer was classified R2 in the Swiss ratings scheme (effectively on the second tier at regional level), which wasn't bad for a thirteen-year-old but still a long way short of the national ratings to which he aspired. That year, he reached the quarter-finals of the Basel Championships, and was making steady progress. But there were worrying signs.

A note from an official Swiss tennis publication from the mid-1990s expresses concern about how the country's most promising youngsters were being handled. Referring to the Old Boys club's greatest prodigy pre-Federer, it reads, 'Emanuel Marmillod is a glowing example of the lack of forward planning. Although the Basler has massive talent and was able to make his way easily to the age of eighteen, he has now suddenly become aware that without the necessary work he won't get anywhere, nationally or internationally.' Meanwhile, another note lists a group of youngsters (including Federer, ironically) and describes them as 'all talents who are prevented from unleashing their potential because the school system or society is not yet willing to accept this working together of education and top-level sport. Something has to happen!'

While Lynette Federer no doubt saw these notes, there's no evidence that the Federer family was in any way influenced by them. They were aware, however, that the 'Tennis Études' programme run at the Swiss National Tennis Centre in Ecublens, on the outskirts of Lausanne, offered a potential next step for the thirteen-year-old Roger. It offered the option of continuing his education in a tennis environment. For someone not keen on going to school, like Roger, it was certainly a possibility.

In March 1995, Roger took the three-day entry test and passed with flying colours, clearly giving the coaches the impression that he really wanted to enrol on the programme. But going to Ecublens would have meant leaving the tutelage of Peter Carter and, more importantly, leaving his family in Basel to live for at least five days a week in a different part of the country where he hardly spoke the language. And he had always professed himself as being very close to his family. He was chugging along nicely at Old Boys, so there was no need to uproot, was there?

His parents were happy to show him the tennis centre and investigate other possibilities for furthering his career, but Roger seemed set on staying in Basel. In the car on the way home from the entry test at the centre, he said to his parents, 'I'm never setting foot inside Ecublens again.'

4

FEDERER ARRIVED AT Ecublens just a few days after his fourteenth birthday and just a few weeks after vowing never to set foot in the Swiss National Tennis Centre. While his decision to enrol on the Tennis Études programme seems to have developed a momentum of its own, it was probably a lot more intentional than that. Shortly after passing the entry test, he was asked by a journalist from the Swiss tennis magazine *Smash* whether he was thinking of taking up a place at Ecublens. 'Perhaps,' he replied, 'you never know.' That quote made it into print. On reading it, his parents – somewhat nonplussed after hearing his views in the car after first visiting the centre – questioned him about it, to which Roger replied, 'Well, it's written there, so I'm going.'

Lynette Federer says there was no parental pressure on him either way. She told the British newspaper the *Daily*

Telegraph, 'We're a close family, but Roger took the decision at a very early age that he wanted to play tennis away from home. His father and I saw our role as supporting his project, to help him develop his own confidence, and to help him if things didn't turn out quite the way he would have wished. As a result, we never forced him to do anything; we let him develop on his own. He made a lot of important decisions himself when he was younger, and that was key to his success. He learned to be very independent.'

By 1995, the Swiss National Tennis Centre was in something of an interim state. In 1992, the national association Swiss Tennis (the English name 'Swiss Tennis' has been used since the 1980s as a single brand to avoid the need to write the German, French and Italian versions of 'Swiss Tennis Association' on every official document) suffered a major internal schism over how best to structure the development of the country's top talent. The upshot was that, the following year, the four regional tennis centres were merged into one in Ecublens, a picturesque town on the shores of Lake Geneva, just west of Lausanne, which would serve as a temporary arrangement until the organisation's brand-new purpose-built centre opened in Biel in 1997. Even the choice of Biel was politically sensitive; although its bid to host the new administrative and performance centre had its merits, part of the reason it was picked was its geographical location, right on the linguistic border between German- and French-speaking Switzerland (hence its frequent representation on maps as 'Biel/Bienne', 'Bienne' being its Francophone name).

The Tennis Études programme was inaugurated in 1993 and was intended to provide the most promising tennis players with the chance to make the most of their talent without neglecting their schooling. When Federer went there, his school lessons went down from thirty hours a week to twenty. The programme was set up by one of the most experienced coaches in European tennis, Georges Déniau, but he fell victim to the Swiss Tennis eruptions of 1992, and, by the time Federer arrived, the centre was being run by Déniau's deputy, Christophe Freyss (responsible for the coaching), and Pierre Paganini (in charge of the fitness programme). After a troubled first year at Ecublens, the centre's reputation quickly grew among the Swiss tennis-playing community to the point where, in its third year, sixty young hopefuls applied for just four places. Those sixty were whittled down to sixteen who were allowed to take the entry test. This consisted of running, a fitness assessment course, demonstration of various strokes and a test match in which an applicant's technique and competitive temperament were analysed.

During his test, Federer so impressed the two heads of the programme that he was offered a place on the spot. Freyss said of him, 'He shows a natural talent as well as a basic technique that has no significant weaknesses, but he will have to work hard physically in the next few months. But it was also an important criterion for selection that Roger left us with the impression that he really wants to come to Ecublens.' So much for never setting foot there again!

When Federer moved to Ecublens in 1995, the centre had a dozen or so youngsters (boys and girls). They couldn't accommodate more than about 15 because the centre had access to only four indoor hard courts, four outdoor clay courts and a small gymnasium, all rented by Swiss Tennis. The students also had part-time use of a football pitch and a running track 100m from the tennis facilities. They had their own accommodation, generally in a studio or shared apartment for the older ones or lodgings with a family for those also attending a local school.

The average day for those based at the centre would begin with a wake-up call at something like 6.30, with school starting at 7.45 and lessons for those on the Tennis Études programme finishing no later than 1pm. The students would then head to the tennis centre for a two-hour practice session, followed by an hour's physical training, before going home for a quick dinner. At weekends, the centre was empty, the occupants either having gone home or – more often – participating in tournaments elsewhere in Switzerland, so any homework had to be done in the evenings during the week.

There were other coaches working at the centre besides Freyss and Paganini – Alexis Bernhard was one who worked with Federer – but Freyss had overall control not just of the programme but also of each player's tournament schedule. With one coach for every three or four players, when the students went to play tournaments, one coach would look after a handful of players. Everything at Ecublens was in the French language, not just the schooling and relations with host families, but French was also the house language of the tennis centre. So, while the handful of kids from the German-speaking part of Switzerland could speak German among themselves, they had to speak French to their coaches and officials.

In an article written by Thomas Wirz that appeared in the *Basler Zeitung* in March 1995 proudly announcing Federer as the first player from Basel to be accepted by the Tennis Études programme, his father Robbie made it clear that the school element was not to be neglected. 'Roger isn't the most hard-working in school,' he said, 'but thanks to the fact that he'll have access to one-to-one advice, and the centre has Annemarie Rüegg looking after the educational side of things, we're not expecting this to be a major problem.' Wirz then ends the article with an interesting observation: 'Federer has now secured his place in the Tennis Études team, and after the summer holidays he will embark on the second stage of the apprenticeship that might soon lead to his becoming a very good tennis player.'

That Federer survived the first few months was something of an achievement. He had only limited French, was frequently homesick, and admits to being close on several occasions to packing his things and returning home. 'For me, the first half-year was very tough,' he has said in several interviews. 'I wanted to go home. I was not happy. I used to cry when I had to leave on Sunday nights to go back.' He told the Swiss journalist Roger Jaunin, 'I was the Swiss German who everyone liked to make fun of.

People were mean to me and it was hard to leave for Ecublens on Sunday nights. Very hard.'

Piecing together tales emanating from that time, he was clearly the butt of numerous practical jokes, including frequent occasions when he entered his name on the massage list only to turn up for his appointment to find it had been erased by an older boy who then took his place. In short, it was bullying.

Federer found release for his frustration on court. Even so, while he was able to express himself through impressive forehands and backhands, the off-court stress hardly made him behave any better, and he became notorious for his racket-throwing. There's a story that, when a new backdrop was installed on one of the courts, Federer was the first to put a hole in it and was punished by being made to sweep the courts early in the morning.

One of the more senior players already at the centre when Federer arrived was Yves Allegro, a player three years older who went on to make it into the world's top fifty in doubles and partner Federer in the Davis Cup and the Olympic tennis event of 2004. He remembers Federer frequently reduced to tears of frustration at the difficulty of coming to terms with it all, phoning home at regular intervals and generally 'having a tough time'. Yet, through that difficult time, he developed a cussed will to stick it out and, while it might be a little far-fetched to attribute his determination to come back from seemingly hopeless match situations to those first few weeks in Ecublens, there's no doubt he learned several lessons which made him a stronger person for the somewhat strange life that was to follow on the global tennis circuit. His mother told the British journalist Mark Hodgkinson, 'It was a great lesson in life for him – that things don't always go your own way, and that you don't get anywhere in life with talent alone. You have to work at things. I know it wasn't always fun and games for Roger there, and that many days he wasn't that happy, but those struggles were good for him. Overcoming those ups and downs were a challenge, and it helped him develop as a person.'

Two things clearly helped Federer get through those first few weeks at Ecublens: tennis and his lodgings. However difficult he found speaking French, and however much he longed for his family and his friends in Basel, he could at least express himself on the court, and some of his former associates at Old Boys believe that the determination that Peter Carter had helped him unearth was instrumental in seeing him through the initial weeks. He also had a temporary family to go home to in the evenings, who clearly tried to make him feel like one of their own. While Allegro had his own studio apartment, Federer was housed with Cornélia and Jean-François Christinet and their three children, Vanessa, Nicolas and Vincent. 'Most evenings we used to mess about – fighting or playing basketball or table tennis,' Vincent later told Roger Jaunin. 'I remember his coaches reproaching him for his lack of punctuality, and he had no excuse. Even on the days when he had exams at school, you had to shake him three times to get him out of bed.'

Eventually, Roger settled down and became happy at the centre, but, until his tournament schedule became too heavy, he would come home every weekend to spend time with his family and his friend Marco Chiudinelli. 'We played very little tennis after he went to Ecublens, but we still used to hang out together,' Chiudinelli says. 'We'd play a lot of computer games, both at home and in arcades in the city. We both had a strong sense of competition, we both wanted to win. I look back on it as a wonderful time, and Roger was a big part of it.'

Federer also continued to be a part of the Old Boys set-up, turning up for inter-club matches until he became world junior champion towards the end of 1998. The work he'd done at Ecublens became clear to his old sparring partners. 'There was one occasion,' recalls Niki von Vary, 'when he was fourteen. He'd just gone to Ecublens and had a national rating. Then he came back to play with us and I was up against him in practice for inter-club matches. He'd really improved, and we could see that he was going to be good. Even so, as good as he's turned out, no one could have seen it at that time.'

Von Vary was also a witness to Federer and Chiudinelli's continuing demon double act. 'On one occasion, Old Boys staged the Basel championship,' he says, 'and during the event Roger, Marco, Reto Staubli [one of Roger's closest friends who today frequently travels with him on the tour] and I were playing cards in the club restaurant. Roger and Marco were so loud that the tournament director stomped in and said that they were making so much noise that the players on the centre court couldn't concentrate. There are other stories about them, but that sums up who they were: spirited, funny and loud, yes, but never malicious. And you had to be on your guard, because they were always up for a prank or a practical joke.'

Looking back, Federer only really began seriously working on his tennis when he went to Ecublens, and again the question arises: were people aware at that time that they had a potential world-beater in their midst? Probably not, because by general standards Federer was something of a late developer. 'Up to the age of fourteen, he was what you might call a normally talented youngster, doing well in junior tournaments, winning some, but realistically not much more,' says the Basel journalist and coach Thomas Wirz. 'For example, at fourteen he lost in the quarter-finals of the Basel junior championships – a regional tournament – which isn't bad but doesn't indicate someone headed for the very top. He was a junior with a good game – no more, no less. Otherwise, he would have been more dominant. His biggest spurt, in terms of results and achievement, came between autumn 1996 and spring 1997, when he was fifteen.'

It was in 1996 that the first signs that people were getting excited about him began to emerge. In the late summer of that year, he made his international debut, representing Switzerland in the World Youth Cup, a team tournament organised by the International Tennis Federation, held that year in Zurich on outdoor clay. When Switzerland were drawn to play Australia, a number of media people showed up for the battle of the number ones: Federer against an exciting young Australian, Lleyton Hewitt.

It was a fascinating encounter in more ways than one. Hewitt was somewhat better known, having made more progress as a junior than Federer, and just four months later he was to announce his presence by winning the full ATP Tour title in Adelaide at just sixteen. Although Federer wasn't working officially with Peter Carter at that time, he was in regular contact with him so was well aware that Hewitt was being coached by Darren Cahill, Carter's former stablemate from Peter Smith's set-up in Adelaide. There was a sense that this could be a meeting of players who would go on to great things, and the match lived up to the billing, Federer winning 4–6, 7–6(3), 6–4, although Australia went on to win the tie on a deciding doubles.

The following year proved to be a pivotal one in Swiss tennis. In January, Martina Hingis became the first Swiss of either gender to win a Grand Slam singles title when she won the Australian Open. By the end of March, she was world number one, and she went on to win three of that year's four major singles titles, adding the Wimbledon and US Open trophies to her Australian success, and narrowly missing out on the French Open when she was beaten by Iva Majoli of Croatia in the final.

1997 was also the year Swiss Tennis opened up its new performance and administrative centre in Biel. Finally, the political infighting of five years earlier could be laid to rest (well, partly; it's never far from the surface in Swiss Tennis) and the small Alpine country had a base devoted to training its top tennis talent, both juniors and touring professionals. With the opening of the new facility and Hingis's elevation to the status of sporting icon, tennis in Switzerland was appearing increasingly attractive, and soon a number of highly respected names were attracted to Biel, among them the Dutch coach Sven Groeneveld and the Swede Peter Lundgren, who was appointed 'National Trainer' there.

Another coach to arrive at Biel was Peter Carter, who had been lured away from the Old Boys club by Swiss Tennis in the summer of 1997, largely because of his links with Federer, who was being increasingly recognised as a prospect worth nurturing. After his eight years of service in Basel, the club held a large farewell party for him, and the collection raised for him went into four figures – a sign of how well liked and respected he was there.

Things were looking up for Federer, too. After two years at Ecublens, he could base himself much closer to home, having mastered French and overcome his other demons. And he had his most trusted coach back with him, with funding from Swiss Tennis. But where was he to live? He didn't want to lodge with another family, but at sixteen he wasn't ready to have his own place.

Enter Yves Allegro. Although he had finished his own schooling in Ecublens, when he turned professional Allegro decided to base himself in Biel and had taken an apartment there. When the Federer family heard about this, they asked him if Roger could share with him. Allegro agreed and the pair became flatmates for two years. 'We had a lot of fun,' Allegro says today. 'We became very close friends. He was close to turning pro, so it wasn't very easy for him sometimes because he wasn't great at waking up at eight o'clock to go to practice and he was late a lot. He used to love playing PlayStation in the evening, and sometimes I had to stop him and say, "Come on, it's time to go to bed now." I was kind of like an elder brother to him.'

Given all the hassles with French that had plagued Federer when he first went to Ecublens, it may have been psychologically valuable for him to have developed a friendship in which the default language was French. 'We always speak French,' says Allegro, 'which is quite strange because by that point my Swiss German wasn't bad. Even today we speak more French than Swiss German together, although now we mix three languages: French, Swiss German and English.'

But what was Federer like to live with? Did he do his share of the washing-up? 'He was all right,' says his former flatmate. 'We weren't too bad. If I told him to do something, he did it. He probably wouldn't have done it by himself but, if I told him, he always did it.'

These days, Allegro's high-profile appearances on the tennis tour are mostly as Federer's side-kick. He has had a successful partnership on the doubles tour with the German Michael Kohlmann, but it's at Davis Cup ties or when he teams up with Federer that he plays before the biggest crowds. So does he find it strange to be the former 'elder brother' who's now the junior on-court partner to one of the biggest names in world sport? 'No, it's not strange. In fact, I think it's a nice story. I'm not jealous at all. I'm very happy about what Roger's doing. I'm doing my stuff and he's doing his stuff. It was nice to win two titles with him and it's nice to play in the Davis Cup with him, just because it's a nice story.'

1997 was also the year Federer gave up on his schooling. 'I told my parents, "I'm not in the mood to go to school any more and I want to focus on tennis,"' he said in an interview in 2004. 'They understood, but they said that if, in the next few years, I didn't have any results, I'd have to go back to school. It was a pretty big risk for me to stop school at sixteen because I didn't have an ATP ranking at that time. Maybe I was 800th or something, and in the juniors I was, like, 60th or something. But somehow I felt that school was disturbing me from being one hundred per cent focused on tennis. That's why I quit school, and then tennis went much better.'

By the time he left school, he had notched up his first tournament success. In January 1997, he became the Swiss under-eighteens junior champion while still only fifteen. Then in May he won the international junior title in Prato, Italy, winning six matches in straight sets against some of the best juniors of the time. But that was to be the only title he won that year, and he still hadn't played in a junior Grand Slam.

So what kind of a player was Federer at sixteen? He has said his graceful style came naturally and didn't really emerge until his late teens, but under the guidance of Alexis Bernhard, Christophe Freyss and Peter Carter he was clearly enhancing the efficiency of the smooth stroke-making Seppli Kacovski had taught him at Old Boys. Thomas Wirz recalls of that time, 'I always had a little concern about his playing style. He always played a high-risk game, hitting very flat, clearing the net by very little, and that made me think at the time that he would never win the French Open. He's added some spin that allows him to play better on clay, but his game still isn't well suited to slow courts. But then, he's always had a very economical style, so he doesn't need the degree of musculature that some players need. He's a bit like Michael Stich in that respect, very efficient.'

And still the volatile temperament was there to haunt him. 'I was throwing around my racket like you can't imagine,' he said in an interview quoted by the website tennis-x.com. 'Helicopters were flying all over. I mean, I was getting kicked out of practice sessions when I was sixteen. I used to talk much more, too, and scream on court.'

His parents tell the story of driving home from a tournament through an Alpine pass. Federer was angry at the way he had played, and was becoming very hot-tempered in the car. His father tried ignoring him, but that didn't work, so he stopped the car, dragged Roger out and rubbed his head in the snow as a symbolic way of cooling him down. 'Roger never heard a bad word from us just because he had lost,' his mother said in an interview with Freddy Widmer of the *Basler Zeitung*, 'but when he misbehaved or when he just didn't make an effort, we weren't going to let that go.'

Lynette is convinced her son gained strength from his bad experiences because of her and her husband's attitude towards him. 'Our son was always allowed to be a bit wild, but he always had to take responsibility for the consequences. If he dug himself into a hole, he had to dig himself out of it.'

This same philosophy was adopted by the Swiss Tennis centre in Biel, where he was once made to clean the toilets early one morning after doing some material damage while misbehaving during a training session.

Yves Allegro certainly remembers the tantrums. 'He'd get pissed off very easily and throw rackets all over the place,' he recalls. 'Not very bad, but often. I think he was even worse in practice than in matches. He was very competitive in matches.' But Allegro also recognises that it was around that time, towards the end of 1997, that Federer began to make the most progress in his game. And, as the new year dawned, he was set to take the junior world by storm.

There are mixed opinions as to how to regard the official world junior champion. For some, the achievement is a stepping-stone to greatness, while for others it can be the opening chapter in a tale of unfulfilled promise. Since the first world junior champions were crowned in 1978, a number have gone on to top the rankings – Ivan Lendl, Stefan Edberg, Andy Roddick, Martina Hingis and Amélie Mauresmo, for instance –

while others such as Brian Dunn, Federico Browne, Zdenka Malkova and Nino Louarsabishvili have disappeared with little trace. They might be the best in the world at under-eighteens level, but, if they're born in a year of few top players or many late developers, the honour might be of little ultimate meaning. The same goes for the Grand Slam junior championships: while they give young players a chance to rub shoulders with great players in the locker rooms and play on the courts they've recently vacated, winning a junior Grand Slam title doesn't always offer the greatest indication of likely champions of the future.

In 1998, Federer played a full year of the top junior events, which include the four Grand Slams and a series of colourfully named tournaments including the Coffee Bowl, the Banana Bowl and the culmination of the year: the Orange Bowl. He won the Victoria Junior Championships in Australia the week before the Australian Open, and then went on to reach the semi-finals at what was then still called Flinders Park (now Melbourne Park).

Playing his first Grand Slam event brought him into contact with the kind of regular media presence that would accompany him for the rest of his playing career. Marco Mordasini is a Swiss radio journalist, who was earning most of his money at the 1998 Australian Open reporting on Martina Hingis and Patty Schnyder, but – like most reporters – was keeping an eye out for any new home-grown talent in the junior events. He spoke to Federer several times during that tournament, most notably after the Swiss had lost a very close match in the semi-finals to Sweden's Andreas Vinciguerra 4–6, 7–5, 7–5.

'I'd asked to speak to him,' Mordasini recalls, 'so, a while after his match had finished, Mitzi Ingram Evans, the player liaison officer for the juniors, brought him into the radio room. At that moment, Hingis or Schnyder had just won and I had to go on air to give the result, so I asked Roger if he could wait a couple of minutes – I explained why – and he said yes. So I sat him down next to me and, as I was waiting to go on air, I heard a snuffling sound. I looked over and there he was, crying his eyes out. He cried for what seemed like about ten minutes about losing this match. I asked him what was up. As I'd seen it, he'd played a superb match; the other guy just happened to be one notch better. Roger explained that he wasn't sad because he'd lost but because he knew then that he'd had the chance to win and hadn't used his chances. He could see what he should have done differently, and it hit him hard. It was a powerful moment.'

Mordasini says Federer was easy to deal with on a personal level, although he needed some coaxing. 'He seemed shy,' said the journalist, 'at times very shy, but always very well mannered, said "Sie" [the more formal or deferential of the German pronouns for 'you'] to me, unlike most teenagers. He was very calm; he didn't speak in torrents. You had to encourage him to come out of himself a bit. It was like there were two people: one on the tennis court, where he knew what he was doing, and the other in the media area, where he was a bit restrained. I told him the rules of my game – that I'd cut out anything he said which didn't come out right – and I think that encouraged him to develop something of a sense of trust with the media – at least with me. Over the years, he's genuinely come out of himself. It's not a PR act that he's learned.'

A third junior title, and the second of the year, came in the springtime in Florence, which helped to raise his profile in Switzerland. One of the many people who took note of his performance was Köbi Hermenjat, the tournament director in Gstaad whose Swiss Open clay court event takes place the week after Wimbledon. Hermenjat judged that, if this young Swiss boy – still only sixteen – could win a junior title on clay, he was worth a wildcard. (The field for a professional tennis tournament is made up mostly of players who are the highest-ranked applicants, plus a handful of 'qualifiers' and 'wildcards'. A pre-tournament competition is held to work out who wins through 'qualifying', and a tournament director has a couple of invitations – 'wildcards' – to give to players who wouldn't qualify as of ranking but who would enhance the appeal of the tournament, eg local players or star names on a comeback after injury. Qualifying tournaments also have wildcards, and Federer was given one for the tournament in Toulouse.)

Hermenjat offered Federer his wildcard, and Federer jumped at the chance. His opening on to the full ATP Tour had finally arrived, a milestone that helped him to decide that 1998 would be his last year on the junior circuit (even though he'd still be eligible in 1999). But, before the Gstaad tournament came round, he had another milestone to reach.

Although he bombed at Roland Garros, losing 6–4, 5–7, 9–7 to the Czech Jaroslav Levinsky, he found his feet on the grass in London. First, he reached the semi-finals at Roehampton, losing to Taylor Dent in three sets, and then went on to Wimbledon, where with barely a volley in sight he won the junior event, beating the Georgian Irakli Labadze 6–4, 6–4 in the final. Then he and the Belgian Olivier Rochus won the doubles title, beating Michaël Llodra and Andy Ram, also in a 6–4, 6–4 final. After all the fun in practice sessions at Old Boys in which he'd said, 'With this shot I'll win Wimbledon,' Federer was finally a Wimbledon champion, albeit in the junior events.

Permit me a personal recollection here. The day he won his Wimbledon junior title was the day I met him for the first time. During the 1990s, I talked to a lot of juniors. Some were cocky, some were shy, some were fiercely ambitious and some were coy about saying how far they could go. What struck me about Federer was a remarkable mixture of charm and ambition. He made instant connections with people, he certainly made me feel he was pleased to have chatted with me (and I know I'm not the only one to have felt this), and he had an arrogance that was in no way offensive. There's always quite a media interest surrounding junior Grand Slam champions – largely as an investment for the future, just in case they prove to be any good – and the clichéd question is always:

do you think you'll win the full title one day? I regret I succumbed to the cliché; in response, Federer flashed his cheeky smile and said, 'Why not?'

I'd love to say that I saw there and then that he was destined for greatness, but I can't. I'd talked to too many juniors who saw their destiny in the world's top ten, if not beyond. What I can honestly say is that he made a bigger impression on me as a human being than any of the others did.

Federer's two Wimbledon titles earned him an invitation to the black-tie Wimbledon champions' dinner at London's Savoy hotel, where he would have been fêted alongside the full singles champions that year, Pete Sampras and Jana Novotna. But he turned it down, after his coach Peter Carter persuaded him that concentrating on his ATP debut in Gstaad was more important than a social event in London.

Federer's ATP debut turned into a third successive 6-4, 6-4 match, but this time with him on the losing side. On a damp, overcast day, he was scheduled to face the German Tommy Haas, but, when Haas pulled out with a stomach upset, in stepped the Argentinian clay specialist Lucas Arnold, who was too streetwise for the tour debutant. And yet Federer's reaction to his defeat wasn't one of disappointment but of excitement; he was buoyed up by the knowledge that he'd created enough opportunities and possessed the weapons to have perhaps even won the match. His confidence was building.

By now, like many other juniors embarking on the

transition to the adult tennis scene, Federer was playing on two circuits: the junior and the lower ranks of the full tour. He was given a wildcard into the Geneva Challenger at the end of August, where again he lost in the first round, this time to Orlin Stanoytchev of Bulgaria, 6–4, 7–6.

In the first week of September, it was off to the US Open, where he had the chance to go to the top of the junior rankings. He went to New York ranked fourth, and reached the final with wins over his doubles partner Olivier Rochus and the powerful Dane Kristian Pless, who had beaten three seeds en route to the semis: Aisam Qureshi, Taylor Dent and Fernando Gonzalez – all players who have since gone on to enjoy some success as professionals. If he'd beaten David Nalbandian in the final, he would have gone to number one, but the sixteen-year-old Nalbandian – a year younger than Federer, which can make quite a difference at that age – worked out how to play the Swiss and beat him 6–3, 7–5.

Federer felt he was too negative in the whole tournament, saying after the final, 'I didn't play my best tennis, I didn't take enough chances.' Having shown his mastery of the useful but meaningless tennis player's answer, he gave a bigger indication of his determined mindset when asked what he could still improve in his game. 'I could improve everything,' he replied.

The Nalbandian defeat was one of the losses which Federer says taught him so much. 'I always learned more from losses, not wins, and losing the US Open junior final was one that made me wake up. I thought, "I've got to work harder," but it was only a few months after the US Open that I really decided to put in the work, and it paid off in results.'

The next pay-off came just a couple of weeks after his trip to New York. Offered a wildcard into the qualifying tournament for the ATP event in Toulouse, he came through three matches to make it to the main draw. A 6–2, 6–2 first-round win over the veteran Frenchman Guillaume Raoux meant Federer had opened his account on the full tour, and another straight-sets win over the Australian Richard Fromberg took him to the quarter-finals, where he was beaten by the eventual champion, Jan Siemerink. He had served notice that he had nothing to fear on the full tour.

Three days later, Federer was in his third ATP event and the one that really meant something to him: the Swiss Indoors, held at Basel's St Jakobshalle. The line-up for the event is normally impressive, and 1998 was no exception; the field featured four Grand Slam champions: Pete Sampras, Andre Agassi, Patrick Rafter and Yevgeny Kafelnikov. When the draw threw Federer into a first-round meeting with Agassi, the former ballboy was set up for his first encounter with one of the true greats of the sport. In front of a near-capacity 8,000 spectators on the first day of the event, he lost 6–3, 6–2, but he knew he'd arrived. 'The road is long,' he said after the match, 'but I've learned a lot in these past few months.' But, as he found out the following week, there was still plenty to learn.

After playing to the packed seats of one of the tour's

most prestigious arenas, Federer went to Küblis, a picturesque resort near Klosters in eastern Switzerland, which was hosting the first event in a four-week autumn Swiss satellite tournament series. The town of Küblis was home to around 500 souls, and very few of them showed up to watch a few journeymen and budding tennis professionals plying their trade in the local indoor tennis centre, whose four carpet courts were out of bounds for the week. Such is the largely unseen reality of the supposedly glamorous pro tennis tour.

After his fêting in Basel, Federer struggled for motivation at Küblis. In the first round he came up against a lowly ranked Swiss, Armando Brunold, and, instead of using the confidence of the Agassi match and his five Toulouse wins to sail through, he lost the first set on a tiebreak. When he went a break down early in the second set, he began just belting the ball, teeing off on everything and missing most. This came to the attention of the tournament's referee, Claudio Grether, who came out to watch the last few games of Brunold's 7–6, 6–2 win. Grether judged Federer not to be giving his 'best efforts', as required by the tennis players' code of conduct, and fined the embryonic Swiss hero $100.

The following day, Switzerland's mass-circulation daily *Blick* had a field day, printing large and colourful headlines to depict the shame of the boy who only the previous week had been portrayed as the future of Swiss tennis. 'It was tough,' says Yves Allegro, who played doubles and shared a room with Federer over the four-week series. 'It wasn't that he wasn't trying, but after Basel he lost the motivation a little. The next day he was in the paper, and he felt really bad about it.'

Yet you can't keep a good man down for long. Allegro and Federer won the doubles in Küblis, and then Federer won the next singles tournament and reached the final in the one after that, finishing first – ahead of Allegro in second – in the satellite standings after the four weeks.

All that time, Federer had put on hold his unfinished business in juniors: the quest to finish the year as world junior champion. But he had three tournaments left, two of them with singles ranking points to collect. It started badly when he lost in the third round of the Eddie Herr Championships, but he then won his two matches in the Sunshine Cup team event (the first against Juan Carlos Ferrero, another junior who was to beat Federer to the top of the tree), and then went to the Orange Bowl in Miami, the most prestigious junior event outside the four Grand Slam junior tournaments.

On that trip, Federer did something that shocked his parents and many others who knew him: he dyed his hair blond. He says today of the decision, 'Actually, I wanted to change my hair colour many more times, but I just kept it to blond one time. I was on the point of colouring it red once, but that didn't go down too well with my parents. The next thing I wanted was long hair. I guess that's a little bit rebellious.'

At that year's Orange Bowl – where Federer exacted his revenge on Nalbandian in the semi-finals and beat

Nalbandian's roommate, Guillermo Coria, 7–5, 6–3, in the final – many photographs were taken showing the glory (or horror, depending on your taste in hairstyles) of the blond rinse. More importantly, Federer was guaranteed the year-end number-one ranking and with it the tag of world junior champion. His invitation to another black-tie dinner – the ITF world champions' dinner, during the second week of the following year's French Open – was guaranteed, but his passage into the higher echelons of the full ATP Tour was not. He'd made an impressive start, but with his junior career now over, the question was: would he join the ranks of Lendl, Edberg and Hingis to graduate from junior champion to world number one, or would he join Dunn, Browne and a host of other talented hopefuls who failed to make an impression as touring professionals? It was a question that took another four and a half years to answer.

5

OBSERVING WHAT MAKES someone successful is both easy and difficult. On the one hand, everything they do contributes in some way to their success, while on the other it's often hard to pinpoint exactly what makes the difference between the top dog and the rest of the pack. And yet it's hard to ignore the little changes Federer made as he left the junior circuit to join the ranks of the big boys.

In his last days as a junior, he enlisted the help of a psychologist. Although somewhat diffident today about recalling the help he sought and received, he said in one interview, 'I was getting too upset, so I needed some help on how to think about different things and how to get rid of the feelings of anger. That's why I worked with the psychologist. I think I've always been told the right things from the people around me – things like how to behave, how hard to work, what to do, what not to do – but in the end it's yourself who has to react and want to put in the effort, and thank God I realised that – probably a little bit late, but in time to change some things. So, after working with the psychologist, I kind of worked on it myself.'

Yves Allegro, Federer's flatmate at the time he was seeing the psychologist, recalls, 'He didn't do it within Swiss Tennis; he went outside and found his own person and worked with him for a few months. I think it helped his tennis, certainly a little.'

Another thing that changed was a tiny gesture, but obviously a significant one. While playing at junior level, Federer had had a remarkable little routine before every point on his own serve, a routine the Swiss radio journalist Marco Mordasini remembers disappeared overnight. 'He would pick up the ball,' says Mordasini, 'take it with his left hand, throw it from behind his back, from back left to front right, then play it back with his racket between his legs before catching it behind his back, all with an amazing speed and precision. It became one of his trademarks, yet around that time it just stopped. When I asked him why, he just said, "That was junior time. This is now." He used to do it before every point, sometimes even while walking to the service line, and with a perfection that was incredible. But he obviously dropped it as part of a change in attitude, probably begun by Peter Carter and certainly continued by Peter Lundgren.'

With his tennis becoming increasingly disciplined, he needed an outlet for his sense of teenage fun, and that outlet seemed to be his hair. Having done the blond rinse on the Orange Bowl trip, he let that grow out and decided to go for the long look, growing it long enough to tie in a short ponytail, supplemented with a bandanna. That became the trademark Federer look, and he kept it until the second half of 2004. Often in the early days, he was asked why he was growing it long, to which he tended to reply, 'I like it this way. Why should I have it cut?'

Most players coming into their rookie professional year end up playing a number of satellite events on tour, effectively the third level of tournaments below the full ATP (or WTA for the women) and Challenger circuits. But Federer played just one Challenger event, in Heilbronn, before graduating straight to the lower level of the full ATP tour, where, thanks to a wildcard, he got into the main draw in Marseille, one of the full tour events on the short European indoor swing in February and early March. In the first round there, he beat Carlos Moya, who was only six weeks away from being world number one. Then, having qualified for the main draw in Rotterdam, he reached his second successive quarter-final.

Such was the reputation he was creating on the tour that he was given another wildcard, this time into the Ericsson Open in Key Biscayne, his first Masters Series event (the Masters Series was still known at that time as the 'Super Nine'). Although he lost in the first round, he was knocking on the door of the world's top 100 just four months into his first full year on the tour.

Then, in April 1999, Federer made his Davis Cup debut.

Normally, a seventeen-year-old playing his first Davis Cup tie will attract some attention but is by and large viewed as one to watch for the future. Not so with Federer's debut. Switzerland were at home to the previous year's runner-up, Italy, in a first-round tie played in Neuchâtel. The current International Tennis Federation president Francesco Ricci Bitti – then president of the Italian Tennis Association – recalls, 'I saw the line-up and thought, "Oh dear, we're in trouble." His results didn't surprise me, because he had amazing talent, but from 1999 to 2003 he was a guy lacking in concentration. It was so easy for him to play that he didn't work on his concentration. He was really up and down, except in the Davis Cup, when he played wonderfully well, because the responsibility for the country gave him more reason to concentrate.'

By April 1999, Italy were in trouble, and for reasons other than having to face the young Roger Federer. The nation that had won the Davis Cup in 1976, at the height of the career of the charismatic Adriano Panatta, had never been outside the competition's sixteen-nation world group, but by the late 1990s they were in serious decline in world tennis. They seemed to use up all their luck in getting to the 1998 final, which they lost heavily at home to Sweden, and by the following April they'd lost two of their mainstays, Andrea Gaudenzi and Diego Nargiso. Nonetheless, they still paraded as their top player the experienced Davide Sanguinetti, who Federer had to face after Marc Rosset had won the opening rubber against Gianluca Pozzi.

In Federer's first best-of-five-sets match, he despatched

the greying Italian 6–4, 6–7, 6–3, 6–4 in a remarkable display of maturity that backed up what Ricci Bitti had feared. 'I was nervous at the start,' Federer said later. 'It was just so different. You're not playing for ranking points but for your country.'

With Rosset and Lorenzo Manta beating Italy's Stefano Pescosolido and Laurence Tieleman in the doubles to seal Switzerland's passage inside two days, Federer suddenly found himself part of a team fancied to go a long way.

With the veteran Rosset, the increasingly confident doubles specialist Manta, who in June 1999 reached the fourth round of the Wimbledon singles, and the emerging talents of Federer and George Bastl, Switzerland had the makings of a useful team. Suddenly, an away quarter-final against Belgium two weeks after Wimbledon seemed not only winnable but a passport to a home semi-final against France.

With Rosset recovering from a viral infection, Federer was promoted to number-one Swiss player for the quarter-final at the Primrose Club in Brussels, with Manta playing second singles. The Belgians themselves had a rising star in Xavier Malisse, who took Manta apart in the opening match. In the second, Federer was favoured to beat Christophe van Garsse, but van Garsse was one of those lowly ranked players who seem to find at least two extra gears when playing for their country. A left-hander with a somewhat unorthodox playing style, he'd previously posted a handful of ranking-defying results in the Davis Cup, and added another five-set victory on 16 July 1999 against the still seventeen-year-old Federer. In the fourth set, with Federer leading by two sets to one, van Garsse needed treatment for cramps, but then Federer also ended up by cramping as Belgium took a 2–0 lead.

Aware that the Belgians had a tradition of being chronically unable to win doubles matches, the Swiss knew they still had a chance, and they took the doubles to narrow the deficit to 1–2. But all hope rested on the Federer–Malisse match that Sunday. As the American journalist Christopher Clarey wrote of the match, 'Though it is undeniably risky, in this era of egalitarianism and injuries, to predict the future in men's tennis, it was tempting to view the match as the first of many between these two in the game's major events.' As it has turned out, that view – shared by many others at the time – has not borne fruit, for, while Federer has gone on to great things, Malisse has been unable to capitalise on his unquestioned talent, having just one Wimbledon semi-final to post alongside Federer's half-dozen Grand Slam titles. But on that summer Sunday on the clay of Brussels, Malisse had the edge and won 4–6, 6–3, 7–5, 7–6, to end Swiss involvement in the Davis Cup in the twentieth century.

Although the Swiss team had performed creditably, the fallout from their defeat was bitter. In the debriefings that followed, it was noted that Rosset's unavailability had probably cost Switzerland a home semi-final against France. This started a period of introspection, leading to a crisis which reached a peak in November 1999, when Swiss Tennis announced that Mezzadri was being replaced by his former Davis Cup teammate Jakob Hlasek. Hlasek himself had said he couldn't see a reconciliation between himself and Marc Rosset. In other words, the Swiss national tennis association had picked a captain whose relationship with the country's top player was not smooth.

Worse still, the association hadn't consulted the players. In sports with large teams, such as football or rugby, a national governing body would find it impractical – and probably unfair – to consult the leading players formally about their preferred choice of coach, but in tennis, where two players – or one outstanding player and a doubles partner – can take a team a long way, failing to speak with the leading players before deciding on a captain can be suicidal. In fact, in most teams, the captain is *in situ* by the grace of the players.

Swiss Tennis's announcement provoked a display of solidarity among the players and elicited the threat of a strike over Switzerland's first Davis Cup tie of 2000 against the newly crowned champions, Australia. That match in February 2000 was first scheduled to take place at Geneva's Palexpo Arena, a venue that can hold over 10,000 spectators. Through fears that no noteworthy players would end up playing for Switzerland, the venue was switched to Zürich's Saalsporthalle, a venue that can just about clear 4,000.

As it happened, the tie against the Australians proved to be a superb spectacle. Federer found himself forced to play, despite his solidarity with those who were threatening to strike, because he was under contract to Swiss Tennis and was receiving financial help from them. As expected, Hlasek opted not to pick Rosset, which upset Federer, who made it clear he wasn't happy with the choice of Hlasek as captain. Hlasek managed to persuade Bastl and Manta to play, but Manta made it clear he was playing under protest. Not a happy team!

And yet, on the opening day of the tie, Federer beat Mark Philippoussis in four sets to cancel out Lleyton Hewitt's win over George Bastl. Then, when he and Manta beat Wayne Arthurs and Sandon Stolle in the doubles, the feuding nation was on the point of bundling out the champions just two months after the Aussies had triumphed in the 1999 final in Nice. But Hewitt – no doubt mindful of his World Youth Cup defeat to Federer in that same city four years earlier – stormed back to beat his former junior rival in four sets in the first reverse singles, and Bastl couldn't quite overcome Philippoussis, the Australian winning the fifth rubber 6–4 in the fifth set.

To have come so close to victory amid such unrest must have given the Swiss hope, but it was a blow to Hlasek's already under-fire captaincy and sowed the seeds for further trouble fourteen months later.

Back on the tour, Federer's rapid rise of early 1999 came to a bit of a standstill for a few months. Six successive tour events all ended in first-round defeats, including his main draw debut at Roland Garros and Wimbledon. He lost at the French to Patrick Rafter, and at Wimbledon to Byron Black. Between full tour events, he reached the semi-finals of the Challenger tournaments in Ljubljana and Surbiton and played his last Challenger event in Segovia, where he lost in the second round to Nicolas Escudé. But it wasn't until he beat Cedric Pioline – France's Davis Cup hero that year – in Tashkent in September and Rainer Schüttler in Toulouse the following week that he went from knocking on the door of the top 100 to breaking into it.

By now, there was very little need for him to play on the Challenger circuit. He followed up his wins over Pioline and Schüttler by reaching the quarter-finals in Basel, before Tim Henman stopped him, and then was a semi-finalist in Vienna, a city that was to become a happy hunting ground for him. He closed 1999 by returning to the Challenger circuit, winning his first and only Challenger title in Brest, ending the year ranked sixty-fourth, a rise of 238 places from his start-of-year position of 302.

At the start of 2000, winning two rounds at the Australian Open boosted Federer's ranking further, and he reached his first tour final in Marseille in mid-February, the week after the politically charged Davis Cup tie against Australia. And who should he meet in that final but the man he'd sided with throughout the tussles: Marc Rosset. It was a highly respectful final, decided in Rosset's favour on a 7–5 third-set tiebreak. Whether Federer wasn't quite ready for his first title is open to question; the chances are that, had he been facing someone he was less close to than Rosset, his will to win might have been a little sharper. Rosset later joked to the Swiss journalist Roger Jaunin that he'd thanked Federer for letting him win, which clearly hadn't been the case, although Federer was particularly pleased that Rosset had won another tournament, the fifteenth and last of his career and his third in Marseille.

In April 2000, Federer announced he'd be leaving Swiss Tennis that autumn. While he might have left under his own steam, the fact that he was obligated to the national association in the Australia Davis Cup tie probably focused his mind.

A successful feature of many national tennis programmes is the help offered to players in their first couple of post-junior years. The Swedes in the 1970s and the Germans in the 1980s learned that many a promising junior career was wrecked because of insufficient help available to ease the transition from the junior ranks to the full tour. So, while Federer had turned professional in 1998, he had remained under contract to Swiss Tennis, a situation that enabled him to practise at the new performance centre in Biel and receive financial assistance from the organisation. But it also gave Swiss Tennis the final say on who coached him, and meant he'd had to play in the Davis Cup even though he'd objected to the association's choice of captain.

Deciding to leave Swiss Tennis was one thing, but who would then coach him? Peter Carter had been lured to the national performance centre in Biel largely because of his links with Federer from Old Boys Basel, but little by little the National Trainer Peter Lundgren came to share the job of coaching Federer with Carter. The arrangement worked perfectly well, but, with Federer now breaking free, he wanted someone to travel with him, and it came down to the option of one Peter or the other.

Biblically, the name Peter comes from the Hebrew for 'rock', and Federer was certainly caught between a rock and a hard place. It was a difficult decision for him because, while Carter was reluctant to travel full-time, having a fiancée who was battling against cancer, he was reluctant to let Federer go. Besides, the bond between Federer and Carter was much stronger – having been built up over ten years – than the three-year-old bond between Federer and Lundgren.

'It was a decision where everyone was sure he was going to take Carter,' recalls Yves Allegro, 'and then he decided to take Lundgren. I was surprised too. It was a tough decision for Roger, and tough for Peter Carter to take.'

Federer says he made the decision on the basis of 'feeling'. Much was said about Carter not wanting to travel, and that was certainly a silver lining for the Australian, who needed to be at his fiancée's bedside over the next year and a half. Nevertheless, he was very disappointed by his protégé's decision. Once it was made, Carter withdrew, although he was to have a future role in Federer's career as Davis Cup supremo in 2002. And the fact that Federer had chosen against him when he left Swiss Tennis added an element to Federer's grief when Carter was killed in August 2002.

Lundgren wasn't everybody's embodiment of a typical coach. He'd enjoyed modest success as a player, reaching twenty-fifth in the world rankings at the age of twenty and making it to the fourth round at Wimbledon and the

Australian Open doubles final. But he'd earned his reputation more as the player who always toured with a guitar and who loved his hard rock as much as his soft backhand. After his playing days ended in the early 1990s, Lundgren filled out to take on the shape of someone not normally associated with top-level sport, and with his long hair and goatee beard he looked like someone more at home on the Australian beaches than coaching a tennis player aspiring to be the best in the world.

Nevertheless, Lundgren was of great value for Federer, just as he had been for Marcelo Rios and would be for Marat Safin. It's impossible to say exactly what a coach should be – every player needs something different, and only the players themselves know if they're getting what they need from their coach. But Federer clearly felt good in the laidback company of Lundgren, Lundgren had the tactical acumen to allow his charge to construct game plans, and he helped him to work on what still lingered of his volatile temperament. With Federer's hair down to his shoulders by early 2000, he and Lundgren frequently gave the impression of being, if not quite elder and younger brothers, then certainly some kind of soul mates.

There was, however, a third 'rock' in the picture. Pierre Paganini had been at the Swiss Tennis national centre since before Federer went there in 1995. Mindful of the rigours of the global tennis tour, Federer appointed Paganini as his personal fitness trainer in 2000, working with a physiotherapist, Thierry Marcante (later replaced by the Czech Pavel Kovac).

Born in 1957, Paganini is a shaven-headed fitness fanatic who doesn't go in for shouting from the sidelines but instead enjoys sweating with his charges. He and Christophe Freyss ran the Tennis Études programme that Federer joined as a fourteen-year-old, so it was a natural progression for Paganini to become Federer's personal fitness guru, working with him about 100 days a year. Paganini made it clear he had to be involved in planning Federer's tournament schedule as well as his diet and physical training. Out of this has arisen a structure to Federer's year, still in force today, that includes three three-week blocks of physical work – one in December, one in April and one in July – with shorter, more intensive blocks worked in between. This gives a general cycle of tournaments followed by recovery, followed by fitness training, then tennis training, and then back to tournaments, recovery etc. The physical work is based around a five-point plan Paganini has worked out for Federer. It involves general fitness training (gym work to improve stamina, strength, speed and agility), specific fitness work (a mixture of gym work and on-court work concentrating on specific aspects, one at a time), integrated fitness work (various on-court exercises based on general fitness and tennis work), specific fitness training (tennis-playing with clear physical goals) and preventative training (involving physiotherapeutic exercises designed to prevent injuries).

In an interview in 2005 for a book published by the *Basler Zeitung*, Paganini said, 'It's an absolute privilege to be able to work with Roger Federer. In the course of a sports trainer's career, you only have such good fortune once. No, normally you don't have the good fortune at all, so I really am very lucky.'

With Lundgren as his personal coach and Paganini as his fitness trainer, Federer had the team in place for his assault on the top level of professional tennis.

6

IT TOOK A WHILE for the new Lundgren–Paganini regime to bring results. Federer had enjoyed a good run in the European indoor tournaments in February and March 2000, which had included his first tour final in Marseille, but as soon as he started playing outdoors the defeats began to outnumber the victories. But, then, Federer's entire career has been characterised by slow but gradual – and remorseless – progression.

With the exception of the French Open, he lost in the first round of all the clay-court tournaments he contested while agonising over which coach to choose: Lundgren or Carter. In Paris, he reached the fourth round, but he did have a moderately favourable draw, and elsewhere he was still losing matches he should have been winning. By 2000, Michael Chang was all but a spent force and had never been too forceful on grass, yet Federer contrived to lose to him in the quarter-finals in Halle, suddenly seeing his confidence in his volleys evaporate after he dropped serve near the end of the first set. He then lost to the Australian veteran Richard Fromberg on the grass of Nottingham, and while defeats to Yevgeny Kafelnikov, Alex Corretja, Lleyton Hewitt and Juan Carlos Ferrero were all forgivable in one still serving his apprenticeship, the one that hit him hardest came in September at the Sydney Olympics.

The Olympic format allows all four semi-finalists two bites at a medal, with the losers playing off for the bronze. Federer sailed into the last four without dropping a set, but then lost his semi-final 6–3, 6–2 to Tommy Haas. He hadn't shown his best tennis but certainly hadn't disgraced himself, and he was strongly favoured to beat Arnaud di Pasquale in the bronze-medal play-off.

Di Pasquale was Federer's predecessor as world junior champion, but the two couldn't have been more contrasting. A flamboyant player, the Frenchman was let down by flawed technique and a body that wouldn't stand up to the rigours of life on the modern tennis tour. He'd beaten three seeded players to reach the last four, but had been stopped by Yevgeny Kafelnikov in the semis and came into the play-off with Federer with several niggling injuries and little gas left in the tank.

Somehow, di Pasquale eked out the first set on a 7–5 tiebreak, yet still Federer seemed to be in charge. He sailed close to the wind in the second set, but, once he'd levelled on a second tiebreak, the medal seemed to be his. Yet he was broken early in the final set, and di Pasquale claimed the bronze – and the biggest smile on the podium – with a 7–6, 6–7, 6–3 win. The International Tennis Federation's president Francesco Ricci Bitti, an unashamed Federer fan despite the requirement of his position for a semblance of neutrality, said, 'It was one of the most frustrating matches as a Federer fan. He was the better player and di Pasquale was injured, but Federer still somehow managed to lose.' The frustration Ricci Bitti felt was to be magnified three years later as Federer seemed to many to be on the verge of squandering his immense talent.

Yet it would be wrong to say Federer came away from the Sydney Olympics empty-handed. An open-minded citizen of the world, he thrives in the Olympic environment and enjoys meeting other athletes. And yet it was a member of the Swiss tennis team who made the greatest impression on him.

Miroslava Vavrinec, known as 'Mirka' to those close to her, had more of a history resembling Martina Hingis than Roger Federer. Born in the Slovak part of Czechoslovakia in 1978, she had taken up Swiss citizenship and met Federer at Biel shortly after the national tennis centre opened in 1997, so they already knew each other a little when they met again in 2000. The previous year, Vavrinec had broken into the world's top 100, and her aggressive net game earned her a call-up to the Swiss Fed Cup team. She was then invited to partner Emmanuelle Gagliardi as Switzerland's entry to the 2000 Olympics doubles tournament and, while they lost in the first round 6–2, 7–5 to the Venezuelan pairing of Milagros Sequera and Maria Vento, Vavrinec had lost something else as well: her heart.

It seems Federer did most of the chasing. 'I couldn't work out why he wanted to talk to me so much,' Vavrinec said later, 'and then, near the end of the Games, he kissed me.'

Just before the end of the Olympics, Federer ran into Mitzi Ingram Evans, an International Tennis Federation player-media liaison officer who had been in charge of liaising between the juniors and the media when Federer was a junior. Federer said, 'Mitzi, wait there, I have someone very special to introduce to you.' He disappeared, and returned a few minutes later with delight and pride. 'This is Mirka,' he said.

The Sydney Olympics signalled the start of a relationship that has been of both personal and practical nourishment for Federer. Vavrinec wasn't his first love (he'd had a steady girlfriend earlier in his teens), but it soon became clear that this was more than a fleeting romance. She went on to become his diary secretary and the force behind the development of his RF fragrance, but she insisted that the two of them knew the difference between personal and commercial matters. For a while, they had an understanding with the Swiss media that they were not to be photographed together. That was inevitably broken, yet the Swiss media have generally recognised that the public's right to know stops at the front door of the house they share in the affluent Basel suburb of Oberwil. 'We now allow ourselves to be photographed together,' Vavrinec told the Swiss journalist Roger Jaunin in 2004, 'but you will never read in a newspaper or magazine what goes on in our house.'

The Swiss Indoors event in Basel is one of the regular features on the global tennis calendar. First staged in 1970, making it older than many events on today's tour, it used to mark the opening of the European autumn indoor season, and even today, squeezed as it is between the Masters Series tournaments in Madrid and Paris-Bercy, it still occupies a place as one of the more prestigious tournaments that fall just below the exalted level of Grand Slams and Masters Series. It's therefore understandable for any professional to want to win it, but it means just that little bit more to Roger Federer. Not only is it the only event held in his home city, it's also one of just two men's tournaments in Switzerland. The other is held in Gstaad the week after Wimbledon, which makes it an impractical event for any player who can reasonably expect to be involved in Wimbledon's finals weekend. Though Federer went on to win the Gstaad title in 2004, the feeling in October 2000 was that, if he were ever to win a title on Swiss soil, it would have to be either the Davis Cup or Basel. And having been a ballboy in Basel's St Jakobshalle and knowing everyone connected with the tournament (his mother used to staff a stand there in the days before he became famous), the Swiss Indoors means more to him than it does to just about any other player.

On the morning of 29 October 2000, everything seemed set for the Swiss Indoors to be the first title in Federer's portfolio. In one of his best performances as a professional, he'd beaten Lleyton Hewitt the previous day to reach the Basel final, a result which seemed to be another small turning point in his career. Strange, then, that six years later, at the height of a dominance of world tennis that only Pete Sampras and John McEnroe can claim to have matched, Federer was still without a Basel title.

Federer's semi-final win against Hewitt in 2000 was one of the outstanding matches of his early professional career. Just five and a half months separate the two players in age, they had played against each other in juniors, they were both spurred on by coaches from Hewitt's home city of Adelaide, and both were very much standard-bearers for their generation. Had Hewitt not matured vastly more quickly than Federer, it's possible he would never have got to number one in the world rankings. But, by the time they met in Basel, Hewitt had won all three of their post-juniors matches, including the four-sets Davis Cup win earlier that year which helped Switzerland lose to Australia by the narrowest of margins.

That allowed everyone in Basel to build up the Hewitt–Federer semi-final into the match of the week – and it was, a classic clash of the home underdog, ranked thirty-second, against the visiting celebrity favourite, ranked seventh. The two players played an outstanding match, which Federer won 6–4, 5–7, 7–6 (8–6 in the tiebreak). The Saturday faithful in the St Jakobshalle stood in admiration of both men, especially their local hero, who had vanquished his opponent.

But the effort nearly broke him. The following day, Federer turned out for a best-of-five-sets final against the Swede Thomas Enqvist, who was in the twilight of his career but still ranked ninth and was still very much able to grind out victories against opponents not steady enough to match his relentlessness. Federer dug deep, and took the match to five sets, but he lost 6–2, 4–6, 7–6, 1–6, 6–1.

By the end of his third full year on the tour, he had broken into the top thirty – he finished 2000 ranked twenty-ninth – thanks to the ranking points gleaned from reaching the Marseille and Basel finals and the Olympic semi-finals.

If timing is everything in terms of tennis stroke-making, the timing of Federer's rise to prominence during Switzerland's tennis adolescence was also perfect. A country with a reluctance to embrace sports that don't thrive on its own territory, it was forced to sit up and take notice when Martina Hingis became world number one in 1997. But Hingis wasn't Swiss-born and, while her immigration at the age of seven came early enough for her to speak fluent Swiss German, the man and woman in the Swiss street seemed to find it hard to truly embrace her. One of the country's most experienced tennis journalists, Jürg Vogel of the *Neue Zürcher Zeitung*, once described her as 'the somewhat different Swiss'.

There was no such reservation about the Basel-born Federer. Just a week after Hingis lost in the Australian Open final to Jennifer Capriati, narrowly failing to add to her five Grand Slam titles, Federer finally won a tour title.

The milestone came in Milan, when he beat Julien Boutter in the final to become an ATP champion. Boutter was hardly a player to instil fear into a still teenaged Federer, but the real work had been done in the previous two rounds. In the quarter-finals, he beat Goran Ivanisevic (who would win Wimbledon later that year) 6–4, 6–4, and in the semis he saw off the former world number one Yevgeny Kafelnikov 6–2, 6–7, 6–3.

And what better place to celebrate than in Basel, where just five days later the Swiss team played the USA in the Davis Cup.

That year, the Americans were a team in transition. Patrick McEnroe had picked up the captaincy after his elder brother, John, had given up the job after one eventful year in which he'd enticed Pete Sampras and Andre Agassi back into the Davis Cup fold, only for both to cry off from a semi-final in Spain that the Americans went on to lose 5–0. The American recovery, which was to lead to a run to the final in 2004, began in Basel.

That weekend in February 2001 was to be Federer's. With his surging confidence, he made short work of the always brittle but immensely loyal Todd Martin – by then thirty and with creaking joints, yet still dangerous on his day – who he beat in four sets before wrapping up Switzerland's victory with another four-set victory over Jan-Michael Gambill. Sandwiched between the two singles was a win in the doubles with Lorenzo Manto over Gambill and Justin Gimelstob, a makeshift pairing who played so badly that it probably represented the nadir of

US Davis Cup doubles fortunes. Perhaps symbolically, it took five minutes for the Swiss team to get the cork out of the celebratory champagne, and it was Federer who eventually prised it from the bottle.

With Switzerland 3–1 up in the five-match tie, Patrick McEnroe gave a Davis Cup debut in the dead rubber to Andy Roddick, who was clearly enthused about competing in the Davis Cup – something that couldn't be said for the good burghers of Basel. The stadium was nowhere near sold out for the weekend, despite the distinct possibility that McEnroe might pick his forty-one-year-old brother to play in the doubles. The empty seats created a lacklustre atmosphere, and no Davis Cup tie has been staged in Basel since 2001 (although in fairness this has been partly due to the unavailability of the St Jakobshalle). It seemed that, while Federer might have won the admiration of his home folk, he hadn't entirely won their willingness to support him.

The next Davis Cup tie – a home quarter-final in Neuchâtel against the French in April 2001 – proved a significant moment in Federer's emotional development. 'That was the first time that Federer showed that he wasn't everybody's darling,' recalls the Swiss radio journalist Marco Mordasini. 'After his first match on the Friday, he stood before the press – it was nearly midnight – and said, "I will not, I cannot play Davis Cup as long as Jakob Hlasek continues in the captain's chair."'

Like many disputes, the background of the falling out between Federer and Hlasek is somewhat complicated, but the fact is that the player never got on with the captain. Why this should be so is unclear, however. Although both are very different characters and players – Hlasek achieved what he did through discipline and sheer hard work while Federer can rely much more on natural talent – they have a lot more in common in terms of mentality and approach to life than Federer does with Marc Rosset, with whom he got on fairly well. Whatever the reason, it was hard going for both parties, as well as those around them. Hlasek brought Peter Lundgren into the Swiss entourage in the hope of understanding Federer better, and by the time they got to Neuchâtel he said Lundgren had indeed been a great help.

Hlasek had also made some sort of peace – more of a ceasefire, really – with Rosset, and both tried to put their differences behind them. When the team gathered for the week, everything seemed to be happy in the Swiss camp – but, as Roger Jaunin wrote in his 2004 work *Roger Federer*, signs of discontent were visible to the sharp eye: 'A team photo was taken in front of the hotel they were all staying at and, while almost everyone had broad smiles, Federer's face wore a very sombre expression. Was he just tired, or was it the sign of a deeper malaise? Behind the scenes, the talk was of Hlasek and Federer no longer getting on – in fact, not getting on at all. The tension was palpable, and the smiles were fake.'

As with the tie in Zurich fourteen months earlier, the unrest bubbling within the Swiss camp contributed to a truly magnificent sporting spectacle. The tie not only went to a live fifth rubber but in total had twenty-three sets featuring 275 games in twenty-one hours and two minutes of play. On the opening day, France's Arnaud Clément beat Rosset 15–13 in the fifth set of a match that lasted five hours and forty-six minutes. Rosset saved eight match points but succumbed on the ninth.

Federer then stepped up against Nicolas Escudé before a packed house in the Littoral Arena. The crowd might have been behind him, but he played probably the worst Davis Cup match of his career to date. By then, the sight of Hlasek repelled Federer; photos from the match show Federer staring into the distance as Hlasek spoke to him at changes of ends. Although Escudé was to become the Davis Cup's player of the year – going unbeaten in five singles and a doubles, and winning the cup for France on a live fifth rubber in the final in Melbourne – and had beaten Federer in the Rotterdam final six weeks earlier, the match was decided by Federer's disappointing showing. Escudé won 6–4, 6–7, 6–3, 6–4, leaving Federer facing the media at around midnight with eyes betraying the signs of recently shed tears.

If Federer feels he can't do a task properly, he doesn't want to do it at all. That explains his statement, 'I can't go on like this. I've been saying for months that I have no pleasure at all in playing while *he* [Hlasek] is there. To lose a match like this, and to lose it in the way I did, is destroying me. It's my career that's on the line here.'

To those within the Swiss Tennis orbit, the situation became known as 'die Kuba Krise' (the Cuba Crisis) –

Hlasek was known as 'Kuba', a modification of his first name 'Jakob', which also happens to be the German word for the central American state.

Was Federer trying to test his power, to gauge the boundaries of Swiss Tennis's growing dependence on him? It's a question many people asked themselves after that weekend. The answer is almost certainly not; his feelings about Hlasek were well documented, and Federer is a man for whom the right ambience is important – indeed, some feel it's the main reason he plays Davis Cup ties. 'I have never thought he was trying to exercise any power,' says Marco Mordasini, who witnessed it all first hand.

Whatever Federer's motivation, something had to give, and Hlasek – a pioneer of Swiss tennis who put Switzerland on the map by reaching the top ten in 1988 and steering his country to the 1992 Davis Cup final – was always going to be the casualty. He fell on his sword in the aftermath of what, despite Switzerland's 0–2 deficit after that first day, still proved to be a highly dramatic quarter-final.

That night, Rosset and Federer had a fervent discussion in the team hotel. Rosset was physically exhausted after his marathon match, but both he and Federer decided that they had to play on for the sake of the fans and their teammates. Dealing with Hlasek could come later. For now, they resolved to embark on a salvage operation, one that was to come within one point of being spectacularly successful.

Despite having had little sleep, Federer partnered

Lorenzo Manta in the doubles on the Saturday afternoon. No doubt pleased to have Federer alongside him after the fireworks of Friday night, Manta played one of his best ever Davis Cup matches. The Swiss pair lost the first set against Cedric Pioline and Fabrice Santoro, but they bounced back to win the second and third sets, only to concede the fourth on a second tiebreak. Federer later admitted that he wasn't sure how the Neuchâtel crowd would greet him after his poor showing the previous day, but they were totally behind him. And their support made a big difference in a 9–7 final set that took the match time to four hours and thirty-one minutes.

When Federer beat Arnaud Clément 6–4, 3–6, 7–6, 6–4 to level the match at 2–2, a phenomenal Swiss comeback was a real possibility. However, the talismanic Rosset was still too battered from his match on the Friday, so George Bastl, who had lost his only previous live fifth rubber 6–4 in the fifth to Mark Philippoussis at the start of Hlasek's reign fourteen months earlier, was thrown in again. He raced through the first set, and then took a 2–1 lead on a third-set tiebreak. Escudé took the fourth, and suddenly the tie that had looked so one-sided on Friday night was into a deciding fifth set.

Bastl had the advantage of serving first. When it got to 4–4, he held serve to put the pressure on Escudé – the Frenchman had to hold to stay in the match. He did. At 5–5, Bastl held again for 6–5. Escudé again served to stay in it.

At 30–40, Bastl had match point. A rally developed.

Escudé went for a big forehand that ended up landing close to the baseline. Someone shouted, 'Out!' and Bastl began to raise his arms in triumph – but then realised it might not have been the line umpire who'd called. He played the shot but had been knocked off balance by the call and spooned his forehand over Escudé's baseline. Deuce.

Whether that 'call' beat Bastl will never be known, but Escudé won the next two points to hold serve, and in the next game Bastl was broken. Although he had a stab at getting the break back, Escudé was never going to lose his serve, and France were triumphant.

After the match, the disappointment in the Swiss camp was obviously great, though tempered by the fact that they had salvaged some pride from the horrors of Friday. They just needed the turmoil to end.

It would be wrong to say that weekend drained Federer; a week later, he won three matches in Monte Carlo, and then two more in Rome in early May. Given his early results (he'd followed up the title in Milan with a run to the semi-finals in Marseille, the final in Rotterdam and the quarter-finals in Miami), he had now joined the ranks of the world's top ten. But for all his talent, he still hadn't found the right way to channel his nervous energy and, as he went to Hamburg for the final Masters Series tournament before the French Open, the safety valve that was keeping in his on-court emotions was reaching bursting point.

7

THE SAFETY VALVE burst on 14 May 2001 in Hamburg. As neither Federer nor Franco Squillari were names that cut a lot of ice with either German fans or global television broadcasters, their first-round match at the Hamburg Masters took place on Court 1, a concrete-laden mini-arena in the shadow of the main Rothenbaum Stadium whose location in something of a wind tunnel means it always seems to attract the worst of the Hamburg weather. As a result, few people witnessed Federer's uncontrolled racket smashing after losing to the Argentinian, but it was caught on camera and remains in the London archive of the company that co-ordinates television pictures of the nine Masters Series events. More importantly, enough footage remained in Federer's psyche for him to learn some far-reaching lessons.

The change in attitude that followed his rattle-throwing

in Hamburg might have put him on the path to securing the on-court composure he needed to make the most effective use of his talent, but it wasn't a complete transition there and then. 'I almost had a problem with being too quiet,' he remembers. 'I had motivation and fire, but I couldn't express it any more, so I was struggling with my behaviour. Maybe I lost some time but, looking back now, it was probably very important for me.'

A run to the quarter-finals of the French Open at the end of May restored some confidence, and then, on the grass of Halle, he looked supremely confident for two rounds before falling to one of the top grass-court players of the time, Patrick Rafter, in the quarter-finals. Wanting more practice on grass, he opted to play the Dutch event in 's-Hertogenbosch, notching up three wins there before running into his old nemesis Lleyton Hewitt in the semi-finals.

While Federer was in the Netherlands, the Wimbledon draw was made, with the name P Sampras at the top. There was nothing unusual in this, Sampras had won seven of the previous eight men's singles titles, but by June 2001 the grandmaster of Wimbledon had been looking increasingly vulnerable. He hadn't won a tournament all year after losing to Todd Martin in the fourth round at the Australian Open and to Hewitt in the second round of his favourite grass-court warm-up event, the Stella Artois Championships at London's Queen's Club. In fact, Sampras's last title had been won on the final day of Wimbledon 2000, when he'd come back from a poor start to beat Pat Rafter in four sets in the last vestiges of daylight. It seemed he was ready to be toppled.

That year, the British were too fixated on Tim Henman to look seriously in anyone else's direction. With Sampras on the wane, it seemed that the great hope of British tennis might finally have found his moment. The projected quarter-final between Sampras and Henman was the talk of the Wimbledon build-up, and the flames were only fanned by Sampras's unimpressive showing in his third-round match, during which he dropped two sets against the unfancied British player Barry Cowan, whose ultimate defeat in five sets proved the high-water mark of his career.

Then, when Henman beat Sjeng Schalken and Sampras beat Sargis Sargsian to reach the fourth round, the Sampras–Henman clash was still on. But, unbeknown to anyone at the time, Sargsian, a likeable Armenian who had come through the American college system to carve out a living on the professional tennis tour, was to be the last man to lose to Sampras at Wimbledon that year, and the second-last ever.

On an overcast Monday on which all remaining singles players of both genders were in action, Federer walked out on to Wimbledon's Centre Court for the first time. As well as preparing to face Sampras, he'd had to become acquainted with certain Centre Court traditions, including bowing to the Royal Box if a member of the British royal family was seated there (a practice since abolished). As the fifteenth seed, he was still thought by most tennis watchers to be too much of a work in progress to beat the reigning champion, and it was generally felt this would be a match he'd end up having to chalk up to experience. After all, to most British watchers the match was just a stepping-stone to a Sampras v Henman quarter-final.

Yet enough people close to Federer had expressed their faith in the nineteen-year-old's ability to beat Sampras, and after taking a first-set tiebreak with some good fortune (a dubious serve was called in his favour, and he profited from a lucky net cord) his confidence began to grow. Federer could have been two sets up but missed six break points in the second set, which Sampras took 7–5. A poor smash from Sampras gave Federer the third set, but Sampras stormed through the fourth-set tiebreak to make it two sets all. The fifth set went with serve until the twelfth game, when Federer had Sampras at 15–40. The Swiss guessed that Sampras would serve wide to his forehand side – and he was right. Federer struck a winning forehand return and promptly fell to the ground. After three hours and forty-one minutes, he'd won 7–6, 5–7, 6–4, 6–7, 7–5 to end the great man's run of thirty-one successive Wimbledon wins, dating back to the start of the 1997 event. It was to prove the only time Federer and Sampras ever played each other.

Ever the conservative statesman, Sampras paid tribute to a man he recognised as having many of the attributes that had taken himself so far. 'There are a lot of young guys coming up, but Roger is a bit extra-special,' he observed. 'He has a great all-round game, like me doesn't get too emotional, and is a great athlete.'

The last person to have beaten Sampras at Wimbledon – Richard Krajicek in 1996 – had gone on to win the title, and on that Monday night of 2 July 2001 there were many who were tipping Federer. But the British had got it right – this was the best year for Henman to win. With Sampras out of the way, Henman played one of his best ever matches to bundle Federer out in the quarter-finals 7–5, 7–6, 2–6, 7–6. The win over Sampras had taken its toll on the young Swiss. Although he refused to use it as an excuse, nor even mention it at his post-match press conference, Federer had strained an adductor muscle in his third-round match against Jonas Björkman, an injury that had got worse in his match with Sampras. That kind of injury needs a few days to heal. At some Wimbledons, the rain gives players that kind of time, but not Federer in 2001. He played on – understandably given that it was Wimbledon – but the muscle strain hampered him in his match against Henman and later caused him to miss several weeks of the American hard-court season.

All the same, by beating Sampras at Wimbledon, Federer had announced his presence to the wider tennis world, and although Henman had beaten him, the message for the British was clear: if Henman doesn't win Wimbledon this year, it might be too late for him, because the interregnum between the Sampras and Federer eras looked like being very short.

And so it proved. 2001 was Henman's best chance, but he lost to the astonishingly revitalised Goran Ivanisevic in the semi-finals in a five-set match played over three days.

After winning the third set 6–0, Henman had one foot in the final, but then several interruptions due to rain allowed Ivanisevic to regroup, and one break in the final set allowed the Croat to shatter British dreams. Ivanisevic's win over Rafter in a raucous Monday final is one of the great romantic tales in modern tennis folklore, so it was perhaps a good year for Federer to garner useful experience, rather than win the title that would have created expectations he was probably not yet ready to handle.

Such was Federer's loyalty to the tournament in Gstaad – the first that ever gave him a wildcard – that he opted not to rest the groin strain he sustained at Wimbledon but instead to play on the clay there a week later. It proved the wrong decision; he won just three games against the tall Croat Ivan Ljubicic, and then found he had to take six weeks off to let the strain fully heal.

At least his enforced period of recuperation gave him time to assess the progress he'd made since his realisation in Hamburg two months earlier. Apart from the emotional gesture of falling to the turf of Wimbledon's Centre Court after beating Sampras, he had been a model of calmness, demonstrating almost robotic unflappability in all his subsequent matches. Yet this wasn't something he was particularly comfortable with. 'I felt like I was walking on a tightrope,' he said in an interview that appeared in Melbourne's daily newspaper *The Age* in January 2004. 'When I was getting upset, I was right away called "the bad boy", and then when I wasn't showing anything I was "the guy tanking" [ie 'to tank' is a verb used in tennis to denote the supposedly non-existent practice of a player deliberately losing a match while giving the impression of trying to win it]. So I really had to watch what I was doing, and… I had to find the way I wanted to be and feel on the court. Maybe I can still show more emotions or still show less, but the right balance will come in the next few years.'

The adductor injury meant the only tournament he played on the American summer hard-court circuit in 2001 was the US Open. As the guy who had beaten Sampras at Wimbledon, Federer was suddenly a marked man. He cruised through his first three matches, winning all in straight sets, and then came up against Andre Agassi in the fourth round. Both had played themselves into an illustrious eighth of the draw; it meant the winner of the match would play the winner of another last-sixteen match between Pete Sampras and Patrick Rafter.

The Sampras–Rafter match consumed most of the public and media's interest, as Rafter had announced this would be his final Grand Slam tournament before 'an extended break', which everyone took to mean – and ultimately did mean – retirement. Sampras won the match to end Rafter's Grand Slam career, so by the time Agassi and Federer took to the court, they were playing for the right to face Sampras in the quarter-finals. And there was no question that the New York crowd much preferred the prospect of Agassi–Sampras to a repeat of the Sampras–Federer encounter at Wimbledon.

Federer was eventually to get the better of Agassi, but, in

their fourth-round clash at the 2001 US Open, Agassi gave a masterclass, showing some of the best form of his career, making Federer pay for every small error and eventually crushing him 6–1, 6–2, 6–4. Agassi won the first five games, took the first set in just twenty minutes and continued his dominance throughout the rest of the match. At one stage, he had the crowd purring with a dropshot dripping with so much backspin that the ball bounced back to his side of the net, leaving Federer stranded.

Agassi's impressive form continued into his quarter-final with Sampras, which Sampras won on four tiebreaks in one of the highest-quality matches of recent years. Having beaten Rafter, Agassi and the defending champion, Marat Safin, in successive matches, Sampras seemed on course for a fifth US Open title, but he was undone in the final by the coming-of-age performance of Lleyton Hewitt, who had continued his quicker development to beat Federer to the Grand Slam roll of honour by twenty-two months. The feisty Australian was to beat Federer to the number-one ranking by twenty-six months.

From the high of his win over Sampras, Federer had been brought down to earth. After beating the great man at Wimbledon, he'd had good reason to hope for enough subsequent wins to enable him to qualify for the Tennis Masters Cup, the eight-man year-ending elite tournament that took place that year in Sydney. But his defeat to Henman and the groin injury had left him with just five matches in two months, and, when he lost to Nicolas Kiefer on a final-set tiebreak in the first round of the

Moscow indoor event in the first week of October, his year was fizzling out.

But there was still Basel. As the beaten finalist in 2000, Federer was hoping to improve on his previous year's performance for the third successive year and, when he beat Andy Roddick 3–6, 6–3, 7–6 in the quarter-finals, his route to victory looked clear. A straight-sets win over Julien Boutter in the semi-finals then set him up for his first meeting with Tim Henman since Wimbledon three months earlier. With his groin strain now healed, with the Swiss public behind him, and without the kind of strength-sapping semi-final that had wrecked his chances the previous year, this was surely his moment.

Henman had other ideas. He'd won Basel three years earlier, taking Agassi apart in the final, and once again he showed his comfort in the Swiss metropolis by turning Federer's dream into a nightmare. The Briton won 6–3, 6–4, 6–2 in a one-sided match that took the sting out of the Basel crowd and left Federer numb. 'I just wasn't there,' he said afterwards. 'I played a bad match. I think I just put too much pressure on myself.' More than that, he was building up a complex about Henman, who had now beaten him in all of their four encounters on the tour.

Although he went into the last Masters Series tournament of the year – the indoor event in the Paris district of Bercy in late October – with an outside chance of qualifying for the Sydney Tennis Masters Cup, a first-round defeat to Jiri Novak killed off that hope and suddenly Federer's tennis year was over. He finished 2001 ranked thirteenth and having won his first ATP tournament – a respectable achievement, and an improvement on his 2000 year-end ranking of twenty-ninth. But it could have been so much better.

Federer's second tour title came in January 2002 in Sydney. The arena in which he'd been so frustrated by missing out on a medal at the 2000 Olympics proved a happier hunting ground sixteen months on when he beat Andy Roddick in the semis and Juan Ignacio Chela in the final to announce his presence as one of the rising stars of the new tennis year. But the Australian Open was to be one of those events that – for a while – created the fear that Federer couldn't hack it at the highest level of the sport.

After straight-sets wins over Michael Chang, Attila Savolt and Rainer Schüttler, the eleventh-seeded Federer came up against Tommy Haas in the round of the last sixteen. Although the German was enjoying the spectacular run of form that would take him to number two in the rankings by mid-May – the highest position of his career – Federer should still have beaten him that day. In fact, he had Haas beaten – only to let his fish off the hook. After losing the first set, the Swiss came back to win the second and third, but then lost the fourth 6–4. But he had the advantage of serving first in the fifth set, in which both men were increasingly battling fatigue. At 6–5, Federer had Haas at 30–40, but then made five consecutive errors to turn match point for him into a 6–7 deficit. Haas – at seventh the highest remaining seed left in the tournament after a first week of carnage among the big names – served out an 8–6 final-set victory. A golden opportunity for Federer had gone begging.

And a week later, he failed to defend his title in Milan. He went all the way to the final, but lost to Italy's Davide Sanguinetti, seriously folding in the final set to lose it 6–1. It was an emotional win for the twenty-nine-year-old Italian, who posted his first career title, and in his home country.

Then came a week that, in retrospect, proved to have massive emotional value to Federer. Switzerland hadn't played a Davis Cup tie since that turbulent weekend ten months earlier in which he said he just couldn't play under the Swiss captain Jakob Hlasek. With the threat of losing not just its best player but the one who single-handedly carried Swiss hopes in tennis's top team competition, Hlasek had no option but to step down in the interests of team unity.

Federer then made it clear he wanted his former coach Peter Carter to become the Swiss Davis Cup captain, but there was a problem: Carter wasn't a Swiss national, and according to Davis Cup rules the captain of each team has to be a citizen of the country he's captaining. In 2001, however, Carter had married his Swiss fiancée and was in the process of applying for Swiss citizenship, so a deal was struck by which he became the head of the Swiss team (under the term 'Teamchef', literally team boss) while Ivo Heuberger – the fifth member of the four-man playing staff – was nominated as captain, with the sole responsibility of sitting on the bench and chatting to the players at changes of ends. This model proved sufficiently successful that the Swiss still use it today, several changes of personnel down the line.

Switzerland were drawn away to Russia in the 2002 first round. For the trip to Moscow, Federer's personal coach Peter Lundgren was allowed to be part of the Swiss entourage. By some accounts, not everyone was happy with Federer's influence on team affairs. The Swiss journalist Roger Jaunin says Michel Kratochvil – Switzerland's number-two player by a long way – felt he was denied any such privilege. Be that as it may, with Carter pulling the strings off the court and Marc Rosset still offering an option in the doubles, the Swiss had a more powerful team than they'd presented for some time.

In Moscow's indoor Olympic Stadium, the Swiss were up against a Russian team desperate to win the Davis Cup. Well, Yevgeny Kafelnikov was desperate to win it, in what looked like being his last year on the tour, and in Marat Safin he had a partner who – if he was on his game and sufficiently motivated – could beat anyone on any surface, other than grass. The Russians chose to play on clay and, when Russia plays at home on clay, the clay is frequently very damp and heavy. So it proved for this tie, but Federer played superbly on the first day to beat Safin 7–5, 6–1, 6–2 to win in one hour and thirty-six minutes.

When Kratochvil took a two-sets-to-one lead against Kafelnikov in the second singles and then served for the match at 6–5 in the fourth set, the Russian plan to play on clay looked to have backfired miserably. But beautiful ball-striker that he is, Kratochvil has often had difficulty in finishing off big matches, and so it proved on this occasion. 'I didn't play defensively or afraid,' he said after the match. 'I went for my shots, but I just lost them.' Kafelnikov won the fourth set on a tiebreak and took the fifth 6–2.

A crowd of 8,000 surged into the stadium for the doubles, and they were rewarded with one of the best displays of teamwork Kafelnikov and Safin ever put together. Federer and Rosset didn't play their best on that occasion, indeed Rosset had a particularly bad day and felt he was to blame for the Russians' 6–2, 7–6, 6–7, 6–2 victory, which was also Federer's first-ever defeat in a Davis Cup doubles rubber. They almost got back into the match after saving four match points in the third set, but then lost it in four. It was no disgrace, but it meant Switzerland's fate was now out of Federer's hands.

All he could do was win his second singles and hope for an unlikely Swiss victory in the deciding rubber. The next day, he played his part, putting in his second outstanding display of the weekend to crush Kafelnikov 7–6, 6–1, 6–1, which threw the initiative back to Kratochvil. Although Kratochvil lost the first set to Safin in just twenty-two minutes, he led 4–1 in the second and had a point for a double-break. But once Safin had won the second set on an 8–6 tiebreak, the mountain proved too high for the Swiss to climb, despite leading 4–2 in the third, and Safin took Russia into the quarter-finals with a 6–1, 7–6, 6–4 win.

After the final match, Federer observed, 'For myself and

my singles matches, there was some great tennis from me
this weekend. I couldn't have expected much more. I
would have loved to win the doubles, but they played very
well. In the end it was just tough that we lost the tie.' One
can, of course, read too much into casual comments made
in post-match press conferences, where emotions often run
high, but the impression these words leave behind is that
Federer fully expected that, in order for Switzerland to
win, he had to win all his three matches. As the British
journalist Neil Harman had written in the Davis Cup
yearbook about Switzerland's win over the USA the
previous year, 'The result might just as well have read,
"Federer 3, USA 2."' It seemed that, at least in terms of the
Davis Cup, Switzerland *was* Federer – but Kratochvil
would have his moment of glory the following year.

It took until the end of March for Federer to play a
consistent tournament from start to finish, and, in the
weeks between the Davis Cup tie in Moscow and his run
to the final in Miami, there were signs that the man was
still being formed from the remnants of the boy. One
salutary lesson came in Dubai, where Federer lost 6–3, 6–1
to the German Rainer Schüttler in the second round. It
was not that he lost, rather the manner in which he lost,
that caused concern. To those watching the match, he
hardly seemed to care in the second set. Most tournaments
below Masters Series level tend to pay either appearance
fees or minimum prize money guarantees to their bigger
names – it's a practice no tournament likes to talk about,

but it's recognised as part of what oils the wheels of the global tennis machine. Federer had been offered an appearance fee for Dubai, but such was his slapdash showing against Schüttler that the tournament threatened not to pay it. After lots of to-ing and fro-ing with Federer and his agents, the tournament agreed to hold the agreed fee, to be paid if he turned up the following year and made the appropriate effort. Federer did turn up the following year and did make the effort, winning the first of three back-to-back Dubai Duty Free Open titles. He had clearly profited from Dubai's lesson.

At the end of March 2002, he finally played a consistent tournament from start to finish: the Nasdaq-100 Open in Key Biscayne, Florida. As well as being one of the nine Masters Series tournaments (ie the level of men's event immediately below the four Grand Slams), it's also arguably the most prestigious. Back in the 1980s, its organisers even hoped it would take over from the Australian Open as the fourth Grand Slam. Although that plan was foiled and the event is now probably sixth in prestige behind the four majors and the year-ending Tennis Masters Cup, it is still an event all the major players turn out for.

That year, Federer had to face two of his bogeymen, Tim Henman and Lleyton Hewitt. Henman was dispatched in the third round (albeit on a retirement), while Hewitt was beaten majestically in the semi-finals. This second victory was something of a prized scalp for Federer. Not only was Hewitt the world number one at the time – and Federer had never beaten a number one before – but he was also on a winning streak of twenty-three matches on American hard courts. Yet the contrast between his game and Federer's proved the Australian's undoing. Hewitt's principal weapon, the ability to run down every shot and wear opponents out, cost him much more energy than Federer's bigger hitting. And with Hewitt stretched to his limit in his first four matches, he went into his semi-final having played more than eight hours, while the more economical Federer had spent less than four. With Hewitt looking tired, a break early in each set sufficed for a 6–3, 6–4 Swiss victory and, with it, passage into Federer's first Masters Series final.

After the match, Hewitt offered his own thoughts on Federer's form. 'I think this could be a breakthrough year for him,' he predicted, 'but whether he's going to get up to the top four or five, that's another question.'

Hewitt, whose gruff on-court manner often hides a highly perceptive tennis brain, knew Federer's strengths and weaknesses, and the remark proved highly accurate: Federer did improve, but he finished the year just short of the top five.

With the jinx players Hewitt and Henman vanquished, Federer found himself up against Andre Agassi in the final. They had played just twice before – in Basel in 1998 and at the 2001 US Open – and Agassi had won both. This time it should have been a five-setter: Agassi took the first two sets, and then Federer came back to take the third and served at 4–3 in the fourth. Until the final, he hadn't dropped serve all tournament and, after being broken three times in the first two sets, he seemed to have steadied the ship. But then Agassi – by then just four weeks short of his thirty-second birthday – showed why he is one of the sport's greatest-ever returners. He broke Federer's serve twice in succession to take his fifth Key Biscayne title in his 700th full tour win.

When Federer speaks today of the matches that served as turning points in his career, he often mentions one that few might consider: his win over Marat Safin in Hamburg in May 2002. Perhaps it signified coming full circle after his ill-disciplined outburst in the German city the previous year. 'It was my first Masters Series win,' he says, 'and probably my second-biggest breakthrough after the Sampras match.'

It had always been something of an oddity that a player who'd learned his tennis on clay was thought to be so vulnerable on the red stuff, although in this Federer isn't alone; Boris Becker and Stefan Edberg both honed their skills on clay (though also on fast indoor courts during the winter months) and it always proved their least favourite and least effective surface. Federer lost his first dozen or so tour matches on clay, and by mid-2002 he needed a tournament at which he could show that he *did* have the game for the underfoot conditions that demand so much patience and fitness. That tournament was the Hamburg Masters of 2002.

His first four wins of the tournament – the first three in straight sets – were against players of proven clay-court pedigree: Nicolas Lapentti, Bohdan Ulihrach, Adrian Voinea and Gustavo Kuerten. He then saw off the big-serving Max Mirnyi in the semi-finals to set up a final against Marat Safin, the who had just gone to the top of the 2002 'Race'. (The 'Race' is similar to the rankings but is based solely on results since 1 January of each year, so it gives a fairly reliable indication of recent form at the beginning of the year.) Two years earlier, Safin had lost a fifth-set tiebreak to Kuerten in the Hamburg final, and the mercurial Russian seemed well set to avenge his defeat to Federer in the Davis Cup three months earlier. But it was to be Federer's day, and one of the best of his year.

'It was definitely the best match of my career,' Federer enthused after his 6–1, 6–3, 6–4 win in barely two hours. 'I thought it would be much tougher, but I played unbelievable tennis. I could risk a lot and the balls went in. It was just incredible. I always had the feeling I could break him.' Even Safin said, 'I thought he played the best match of his life.'

Winning the Hamburg Masters revolutionised Federer's clay-court status. He was suddenly installed as one of the favourites for the French Open. But he had yet to learn to deal with the pressure of expectation, and in Paris he froze in the first round against the highly gifted but frustratingly erratic Moroccan Hicham Arazi. Twice a quarter-finalist at Roland Garros, Arazi went into every match knowing he was probably ahead of his opponent on natural ability, even if he let himself down on discipline. Against Federer he was arguably only equal on natural ability and inferior on discipline, but he still ran out a 6–3, 6–2, 6–4 winner. 'I was hoping for so much from this tournament,' Federer said sadly after his defeat, 'but I put too much pressure on myself.'

At least there were still the grass-court tournaments to come. Federer put in his usual appearance in Halle, and looked best placed to win the title, but he came up short over the finals weekend, this time to Nicolas Kiefer, 6–4 in the third set of their semi-final. He then managed to get three more batches of match practice on grass before losing in the quarter-finals of 's-Hertogenbosch to Sjeng Schalken.

Next stop was Wimbledon, to which Federer returned in 2002 with the confidence of the previous year's win over Sampras still ringing in his ears. When he was put on Centre Court for his first-round match against the Grand Slam debutant Mario Ancic, he looked set for a comfortable win, but the big-serving eighteen-year-old from Croatia showed phenomenal composure to deliver a stunning 7–3, 7–6, 6–3 defeat that sent Federer home before he'd barely finished unpacking. Ancic later revealed that his tactics had come from the reigning champion Goran Ivanisevic – they had been merely to avoid the big Federer forehand and attack the second serve. So simple.

'It was a shocker,' said Federer pithily, scarcely concealing his anger. Had he known it would be his last defeat at Wimbledon for several years it would no doubt have been easier to take, but such things seem scarcely plausible in the immediate aftermath of such a frustrating defeat. Instead of Federer, it was his Davis Cup colleague

George Bastl who made the Swiss tennis headlines at that Wimbledon, stunning Pete Sampras in the second round in five sets to draw a somewhat patchy close to the American's glorious Wimbledon years.

Back on the clay in Gstaad, Federer showed how easy it should have been in Paris by dispatching Hicham Arazi 6–4, 6–3 in the first round, but the following day he was again inconsistent against another gifted but erratic player, Radek Stepanek. It was time for a holiday and some fitness work before the American summer hard-court swing. But that season began badly, and swiftly got worse.

On 1 August 2002, Switzerland's national day, Federer lost 7–6, 7–5 in the first round of the Toronto Masters to the muscular Argentinian Guillermo Cañas, who went on to win the tournament. But the disappointment of defeat was as nothing compared to the news that greeted him when he arrived back in the locker room after the match: Peter Carter had been killed in a car crash while on his honeymoon in South Africa.

8

PETER CARTER HAD met his wife, Sylvia von Arx, in Basel. She was a receptionist at the Paradies indoor tennis facility owned by the Basel sports and entertainment impresario Roger Brennwald. Shortly after they'd got to know each other, she had been diagnosed with a brain tumour. For a long time the prognosis didn't look good, but in 2001 her condition began to improve. That year they got married, but decided to delay their honeymoon until she was fully fit and they could have the holiday of a lifetime.

In late 2001, Sylvia was finally given a clean bill of health, and the pair arranged a trip to South Africa as a combined honeymoon and celebration of her recovery the following summer. They were touring in the Kruger National Park in separate four-wheel-drive cars, when the driver of the one Carter was in lost control, and the vehicle plunged off the road near Gravelotte. Carter and the driver were both killed instantly when the roof of the vehicle was crushed.

When Federer came off court in Toronto, his coach Peter Lundgren – the man he had opted for ahead of Carter when he had to choose between them in early 2000 – rang him to break the news. For a while, Federer couldn't believe it. 'I'm very shocked and very sad,' he said in his first public statement. 'He was a very close friend. This is the first time a close friend of mine has died. He wasn't my first coach, but he was my real coach. He knew me and my game, and he was always thinking of what was good for me.'

Eventually, he and Lundgren decided Federer should play the following week's Masters Series event in Cincinnati, and then fly back to Switzerland for the funeral. Needless to say, he was in no fit state of mind for Cincinnati, and crashed out against Ivan Ljubicic in the first round.

After the funeral, he honoured his commitment to play in Long Island, a small tournament just outside New York City which always acted as a curtain-raiser for the US Open, but again he lost in the first round, this time to Nicolas Massú. At least he salvaged something at the US Open, winning three rounds, but his mind still wasn't fully on the job, and Max Mirnyi beat him in straight sets in the fourth.

Speaking now, Federer says of Carter, 'He was a very important man in my tennis career, if not the most important. I had been with him from ten to fourteen years old, and then again from sixteen till twenty, so I knew him very well. He gave me a lot in terms of his personality, in terms of technique and on the court. It was a hard loss. In those weeks after he died, everything went very quickly. I decided that I would compete in the US Open because I guessed that that was what Peter would have liked to see me do, not just to sit around. I don't know if it was for good or for bad... It was also a very influential moment in my career. It certainly marked me, and there was a reaction in terms of how I look at life now. It was a hard moment, and I think of him very often still.'

In the months that followed, Federer frequently had to suppress tears. But the grief made him stronger. In an interview with the Melbourne newspaper *The Age* in January 2004, he said the period pulling himself together after the shock of Carter's death was one of the most crucial in his tennis maturity. 'I guess it made me strong mentally, and I started thinking,' he said. 'I suddenly had time to ask myself, "What do I need to do to get to the next level?"'

Federer's first commitment after the US Open had a poignancy about it that could have brought his grief-blighted tennis right back. But the opposite happened – he played three of his best matches of the year.

After losing to Russia in the first round of the Davis Cup earlier that year, Switzerland were drawn away to Morocco in a tie they had to win in order to maintain their membership of the 16-nation elite Davis Cup world group.

At the time of his death, Swiss Tennis had been confident Carter would be granted his Swiss citizenship in time for the trip to Casablanca; that would have enabled him to assume the role of Swiss captain and thus sit on the bench coaching his players at changes of ends. But, with Peter Lundgren acting as temporary team supremo and Marc Rosset now promoted to captain, the tie became something of a homage to Carter. The Swiss team was united as never before, any unrest put aside for the tough assignment on clay in the heat of North Africa. At the official ceremony, all the Swiss players had their names on the backs of their shirts, but Federer and Rosset had Carter's name as well as their own. As the Swiss national anthem was played before play on the Saturday, Federer's eyes were moist with emotion. It was that kind of occasion.

When Younes el Aynaoui beat Michel Kratochvil in straight sets in the first rubber, the spotlight was on Federer, who faced Hicham Arazi, the man who had bundled him out of the French Open. On his least favourite surface, it could have proved too much for the still just twenty-one-year-old Swiss. But, if he froze under the pressure of expectation in Paris, he flourished under the opportunity to make a statement for his deceased friend in Casablanca. He crushed Arazi for the loss of just six games, playing as if in a trance and admitting afterwards that he felt the key was for him to be in 'a very good mental state'.

The trance continued into the doubles, in which Federer and George Bastl conceded just nine games in beating

Younes el Aynaoui and Karim Alami, and in the first reverse singles el Aynaoui achieved no more against Federer than the six games his teammate had posted two days earlier. It was awesome stuff and, as the Swiss journalist Roger Jaunin reported, el Aynaoui recognised it as such. One of the game's most humane characters, the Moroccan gatecrashed the Swiss celebration party on the Sunday night to say to Federer, 'What you have done this weekend no one else but you could have done.'

Federer dedicated his first victory and his first tournament title after Carter's death to his former coach and mentor. The first victory was a four-sets passage to the second round of the US Open against Jiri Vanek, while the first title came in early October in Vienna. The weekend in Casablanca had restored the on-court confidence that now went with the off-court lessons in life Federer had learned since 1 August. He reached the quarter-finals in Moscow, and then won his fourth career title, the CA Trophy in Vienna, beating Carlos Moya in the semi-finals and Jiri Novak in the final.

The rest of the year continued in a similar vein, putting Federer in a position where, despite his barren fourteen-week spell from Hamburg to the US Open, during which he won just seven out of fourteen matches, he qualified for the first time for the elite eight-man Tennis Masters Cup, that year staged in Shanghai. His consistency at the start and end of 2002 allowed him to finish the year ranked sixth – another major improvement. But the two titles that had really mattered to him – the Swiss Indoors and the

Tennis Masters Cup – were both won that autumn by players who continued to exercise something of a hold over him.

In his fifth assault on his home tournament, Federer managed to reach the semi-finals of the Swiss Indoors, again beating Andy Roddick in the quarter-finals. Everything seemed set for a final featuring the local boy and the French Open runner-up Juan Carlos Ferrero, but neither made it to the final; Federer was taken out in the semis by David Nalbandian, who had beaten him in the US Open boys' final in 1998 and who had yet to lose to Federer since their junior days, while Ferrero lost to another alumnus of the 1998 junior year, Fernando Gonzalez. Nalbandian's win over Gonzalez in the final cut very little ice with the aficionados in the St Jakobshalle!

And then, having battled through the round-robin stage of the Tennis Masters Cup, with wins over Ferrero, Jiri Novak and Thomas Johansson, Federer lost a high-quality semi-final to Lleyton Hewitt, the Australian winning 7–5 in the third set as he became only the fourth man since computer rankings began in 1973 to go a full calendar year in the number-one slot.

Nalbandian was also to have a say in Federer's first major outing of 2003. Having cruised into the fourth round of the Australian Open, the Argentinian was there to put a frustrating stop to the run, again in the fourth round. Four times Federer had played the first Grand Slam event of the year, and four times he'd got stuck halfway – twice in the third round and twice in the fourth. After his five-sets defeat to Tommy Haas the previous year, it was another five-setter, Nalbandian winning the fifth 6–3 to make his record against Federer three wins in three tour matches.

2003 was to be Switzerland's best year in the Davis Cup since the two-man team of Marc Rosset and Jakob Hlasek took the country to its first final in 1992. And it started with a sign that the Swiss team of 2003 might be more than a one-man band.

The Swiss were drawn away to the Netherlands, and the Royal Dutch Lawn Tennis Association opted to play the tie in a corner of the Gelredome football stadium used by the top Dutch football club Vitesse Arnhem. The stadium not only had a retractable roof, but its grass pitch was on wheels, so it could be rolled out of the stadium for non-football events, or for a bit of fresh air during the week. When the grass was in the stadium, the venue had an extra car park.

To history scholars, the city of Arnhem is best known for being the site of one of the bloodiest battles of the Second World War, when British troops looking to set up a bridgehead on the Rhine were shot down in their thousands in 1944. And the Davis Cup tie played there in February 2003 was one of the bloodiest in the 103-year history of tennis's premier team competition.

Before Federer had taken to the court, there was uproar in the stadium, and Rosset – who had been confirmed as Switzerland's captain after the emotions of Peter Carter's death had died down – had kicked a refrigerator in frustration. The Swiss number two, Michel Kratochvil, had battled impressively to come back from two sets down against the solid Dutch number one, Sjeng Schalken, but in the final set a small band of Dutch supporters unused to Davis Cup etiquette became increasingly loud and unruly. When Schalken had match point at 5–4, some of them threw celebration balls on to the court, only to find their hero hadn't yet won. Kratochvil saved a second match point, but on the third one of the troublesome supporters screamed during Kratochvil's second-serve ball toss, causing the Swiss to double-fault the match away. The visitors were furious. Rosset and Kratochvil railed at the umpire, Javier Moreno, and the referee, Brian Earley. As Rosset vented his spleen by delivering a massive kick to the courtside drinks fridge, the atmosphere became decidedly tense.

Into it stepped the man who as a boy had been unable to control his temper. But not any more. Federer kept his head down between points, and kept the points to a minimum in a 6–2, 6–1, 6–3 win over the dangerous though inconsistent Raemon Sluiter. It was his sixth successive Davis Cup singles win and his third consecutive victory for the loss of just six games.

There was some talk in the Swiss camp of Rosset leaving the bench to partner Federer in the doubles, but, having seen Federer team so well with George Bastl against Morocco, Rosset stuck to his role as captain and left the work to his pairing from Casablanca. It was not to work a second time. Against the veteran Paul Haarhuis and the

Davis Cup debutant Martin Verkerk, the Swiss took the first set but then faded in the second, third and fourth, Federer playing one of his least distinguished doubles matches. He almost gave the impression of being depressed on court; when asked about it after the match he snapped, 'Bad question! I wasn't at all.'

Once again, the Swiss squad were in a position where their fate no longer hung entirely in Federer's hands. He certainly wasn't expected to lose to Sjeng Schalken in his next match and, while the match was no formality, his 7–6, 6–4, 7–5 victory was a fair reflection of the two players. 'I played better and better,' said Schalken after the match, 'but Roger does that to me – he brings out the best in me. But then he proved himself even more.'

Federer had done his bit, but now he had to watch as Kratochvil again held Switzerland's fate in the decisive rubber. This was his sixth live Davis Cup match, and he had yet to win one. After Verkerk's impressive showing in the doubles, the Dutch captain, Tjerk Bogtstra, opted for him over Sluiter for the final match. It looked a good choice when Verkerk had set points at 5–0 after less than twenty minutes of play, and Kratochvil looked a fish out of water. But the Bernese son of Czech immigrants, who had grown up at a tennis centre run by his dad called TC Flamingo, put both feet on the ground to score the biggest single win of his career in one of the most raucous environments ever seen for a tennis match.

During the second set, Kratochvil just about held his own and went on to sneak it on a 7–5 tiebreak, winning four points on the run to make good a 3–5 deficit. He then held his nerve in a second-set tiebreak that involved five contentious line calls, two overrules and a set point played with a noise level more commonly associated with basketball than tennis.

Verkerk had two set points at 6–4, but Kratochvil saved both. With the Swiss serving at 7–6, the home crowd were still protesting about a call. Kratochvil waited for quiet. It never came. So, following a nod from the umpire Roland Herfel, who clearly hoped that starting the point would quieten the spectators, he served.

The Dutch thought the serve was out, but Verkerk played it, and a rally ensued.

The noise continued.

Then Verkerk made an error, Kratochvil took the set, the Dutch went wild with anger, and Bogtstra began climbing the umpire's chair in rage. But the point stood, and Kratochvil led by two sets to one, despite having been outplayed for most of the match. From then on, Verkerk was a broken man, and Kratochvil raced through the fourth set for a 1–6, 7–6, 7–6, 6–1 win that saw Switzerland into the quarter-finals.

What Federer thought of it as he sat by the court watching is anyone's guess. He made all the right noises afterwards, two months later he was to say Rosset had fostered 'a wonderful team spirit', and he was obviously pleased to have another chance of glory, one he was to seize in spectacular fashion in the quarter-finals. But it's never easy for someone used to being the undisputed hero to sit back and let a lesser teammate take the applause, even someone as balanced and OK with himself as Roger Federer. Whatever his inherent good manners and sense of team unity had taught him to say that night, there must have been a tiny bit of discomfort in the realisation that this was someone else's moment.

There was no question that Federer was the undisputed hero of Switzerland's quarter-final win away to France. Some veteran tennis watchers even described it as the most remarkable individual performance in the Davis Cup – high praise indeed from those who saw Björn Borg and Boris Becker take Sweden and West Germany to team triumphs largely single-handedly. In the aptly named Zenith Stadium in Toulouse, Federer reached one of the peaks of his career, beating Nicolas Escudé and Fabrice Santoro in the singles, and teaming up with Rosset to scoop victory in the doubles.

In retrospect, the opposition Federer faced that year in Toulouse might not have been of the highest order, but playing France in the Davis Cup is always a tricky proposition. The French have a joker in the pack, an extra card to play, in the form of their captain, Guy Forget. The mild-mannered left-hander has somehow managed to get his teams to be greater than the sum of their parts and has captained a team to three finals without ever having a player regularly in the top ten. Before the quarter-final began, Forget observed, 'Roger Federer is a very good player, and he can cause us some concern, but he's not unbeatable. The simple art of piling the pressure on the opposition while at the same time letting your own players know they can win.'

Federer was more than up for the task. Again he had to steady the Swiss ship after a defeat in the opening singles, but this time it wasn't Kratochvil flying the Swiss flag but George Bastl. Instead of propelling him into a confidence-laden surge up the rankings, Kratochvil's win in Arnhem was followed by a serious knee injury that required surgery, and he missed several months of 2003. Bastl replaced him, but was no match for France's Sébastien Grosjean in the first singles. Yet Escudé, who had beaten Federer two years earlier in Federer's worst-ever day in the Davis Cup, was no match for the man now in the world's top five, Federer notching up a 6–4, 7–5, 6–2 win, despite a slow start.

The agonising in the Swiss camp that Friday night concerned who would partner Federer in the doubles. The choice was between his old friend from childhood days, Yves Allegro, who had yet to play a Davis Cup rubber, and the thirty-two-year-old Rosset. The decision was made easier by an appointment made at the start of the year. The experienced French coach Georges Déniau has many connections with Switzerland, dating back to his days coaching Jakob Hlasek. After being appointed captain, Rosset brought in Déniau as one of his backroom team, and that night in Toulouse Déniau was instrumental in persuading Rosset to take to the court with Federer.

The gamble worked. Rosset played what he described as 'my best match since... an eternity!', he and Federer posting a 6–4, 3–6, 6–3, 7–6 win against Escudé and Santoro, the pair who had won the doubles in the Davis Cup final against Russia four months earlier. After the match, Rosset confessed, 'I didn't sleep or eat last night because I was so nervous to get on to the court. But Roger is a great doubles player; he helped me tough it out psychologically, and this is a wonderful win for the Swiss team.'

In beating Bastl on the Friday, France's top player Grosjean had pulled a thigh muscle, and couldn't play. Forget threw in Santoro, knowing his unorthodox game might cause problems for Federer. It had on several occasions – only six months earlier Santoro had beaten Federer in similar conditions in Madrid, and Santoro had won their first meeting in 1999 which happened to be in Toulouse. But the Santoro wizardry was not going to work this time; Federer was relentless, and the Frenchman won just three games as Switzerland moved through to the semi-finals with their fifth consecutive away win. The semi-final was also to be away, against Australia at the home of the Australian Open. It was to be another tie rich in great tennis, drama and emotion.

In sport and other disciplines such as music and dance, there is a phenomenon whereby some highly gifted players find it tough to reach the very top – footballers who are giants in the club game but can't get comfortable in the national team, or runners who beat the best in Grand Prix meetings but who freeze at the Olympics and world championships, and golfers who on the tour hit round after round below par but who miss the crucial chips and putts in the majors. Similarly, numerous musicians and dancers offer scintillating performances in unpressured situations but can then lose something of their lustre on the biggest stages. All join the ranks of the nearly-men and nearly-women who look like getting to the top but never quite make it.

That was the prospect facing Roger Federer after the first few months of 2003. His form on the tour had gone up to another level, landing him titles in Marseille, Dubai and Munich – none of them massively prestigious events on their own, but thanks to those wins, together with reaching the semi-finals in Rotterdam and the fourth round in Miami, he'd climbed into the world's top five. Among those who ply their trade writing and broadcasting about tennis, the general view was that he was probably heading for the top but he was taking a devil of a long time getting there.

A little irritation – understandably – seeped out at a press conference when he was once again asked about getting to number one. 'I believe I will get there one day,' he said politely yet through somewhat gritted teeth, 'and, when I do, I'm a bit concerned that I won't get the credit for it, because people will have said for so long that I'm going to get there.'

As it happened, he needn't have worried; such was the elegance of his play and the dominance he showed when he finally made it to the top of the rankings that people couldn't help but give him the credit. And the fact that he had appeared to stumble so much en route to the pinnacle probably added to the public's appreciation of his success.

There was another unofficial school of thought at that time, which can best be summed up as 'he'd be better if he wasn't so good'. Behind the obvious illogicality of the statement lay a belief among some that he was so gifted and had so many options on the tennis court that he couldn't work out the right options at the right time. Seasoned tennis watchers know that gifted and all-court players take longer to mature, often because it takes them longer to assemble the experience of putting more components together, unlike baseliners, who have fewer options and so are surer of what they should be doing. But then many gifted all-court players never quite put it all together, and this was the quiet fear behind where Federer stood approaching the mid-point of 2003.

A fourth title of 2003, and a second clay-court Masters Series shield, seemed on the cards when Federer reached the final in Rome in May, beating some quality clay-courters en route. In that final he came up against the revitalised Felix Mantilla, a twenty-nine-year-old former French Open semi-finalist whose best days were behind him. It seemed a formality that Federer would win. But the old demons returned.

Mixing the pace of his groundstrokes, Federer made all the early running but then failed to convert his seven break points and lost the first set. In the third he had three set points but ended up losing the tiebreak 12–10 and, with it, the two-hour-and-forty-one-minute final, leaving the unseeded Mantilla somewhat astonished and tearful, having won 7–5, 6–2, 7–6. Federer had created seventeen break points but had converted just three of them.

A defeat in a tournament final offers no immediate escape – no rushing off court, no quick exit to dodge the cameras and seek sanctuary in the locker room. While the winner cavorts around the stadium in his or her moment of triumph, the loser has to sit there, waiting for the presentation ceremony, working out what nice things to say through the disappointment of a match that has just got away.

When Federer finally got back on to the court, he found himself at the end of a long line of dignitaries, the last of whom was Francesco Ricci Bitti, the International Tennis Federation's president and one of Federer's greatest fans. 'I found myself standing next to Roger,' recalls Ricci Bitti, 'so I took the liberty of saying a few words to him. I said, "Roger, I don't think you should be losing this kind of match. You have to start winning this kind of match, or this is going to become sad for you and sad for tennis." It was totally the wrong moment to say something to him, but I am such a fan of his that I couldn't control myself saying something. Some players would have thought it very bad, but Roger was polite enough to accept it, and that restrained reaction impressed me greatly. He's a very sensitive guy but very controlled.'

Mantilla made a comment after the match that to some seemed to sum up where Federer might be failing. 'I believe I won today because I had the hunger,' he said. 'I played with heart and courage and everything I had.' Was that what Federer wasn't doing? In truth, no. Federer was working very hard away from the public gaze, and was to a certain extent suffering from the curse of the gifted performer: it always looks so easy that the hard work put in behind the scenes doesn't show.

The following week was the Hamburg leg of the Masters Series, and Federer proved somewhat touchy when asked if he thought he was playing too much tennis and thereby jeopardising his chances at the French Open. Even after losing in the third round to Mark Philippoussis, he declined to take any comfort in the fact that his defeat effectively gave him ten days rather than seven in which to prepare for Paris. Hamburg, it seemed, was becoming a place of contrasting emotions for him, with his smashed racket in 2001, his victory in 2002, and now a slightly edgy run-up to Roland Garros 2003.

In most people's eyes, after his first round defeat in 2002 to Hicham Arazi, he was due a reasonable run at the French. And the draw was kind to him, or so it seemed. Seeded fifth, in the first round he came up against the sixty-seventh-ranked Luis Horna, a player who attracts that unkind and dishonest epithet of the 'tennis journeyman'. The match was scheduled for the main Philippe Chatrier Arena at the start of the first day. A couple of hours beforehand, Federer had been given the customary chance to hit on the greatest clay-court arena in the world, but instead of grooving his strokes he flicked the ball casually around and never looked fully focused. Not that this seemed to matter when he led by a break early in the first set. But Horna broke back, Federer's angst set in as the first set wore on and, once he had lost it on a tiebreak, his self-belief ebbed away. Though a hardened clay-courter from Peru, Horna was making his Roland Garros debut, and playing his first match since becoming a father a couple of weeks earlier. Surely Federer would come back. But the second set rattled past and, while Federer made a better fist of it in the third set, he lost another tiebreak, allowing Horna to walk away victorious after just 131 minutes of play by almost exactly the same score by which Mantilla had beaten Federer in Rome.

'I played a poor match and he played well,' was Federer's assessment through the disappointment. 'And, when those two combine, it doesn't help my cause.'

For the second year running, Federer had fallen at the first hurdle in Paris. He was becoming known as a colossus on the tour but with a growing question mark about his ability to perform in the biggest tournaments. Was he the real deal, or was the great Swiss talent flattering to deceive?

9

WITH THE BENEFIT of hindsight, it's hard to imagine that Federer was still very much an unproven quantity as he arrived at Wimbledon in 2003. His victory over Pete Sampras was two years back, he had lost to Mario Ancic in the first round the year before, and for the second year running he was coming to southwest London fresh from a first-round defeat at the French Open. Since beating Sampras in 2001, he hadn't got past the fourth round of any of the four Grand Slam events.

At least he'd notched up his first grass-court tournament. That came in Halle, but even there he'd come very close to losing his semi-final against Mikhail Youzhny, and in the ten previous stagings of the Gerry Weber Open, the best the Halle champion had done at Wimbledon was the fourth round. According to Gerhard Weber, the women's clothing magnate who launched the Halle tournament in

1993, the idea was that 'Wimbledon starts in Halle'. Yet the failure of those who had done well in Halle to go on and do well at Wimbledon was beginning to undermine the reliability of the Halle event to indicate pre-Wimbledon form. By 2003, Weber was becoming desperate for the champion of his tournament to go on to win Wimbledon – but in his 2003 champion he finally seemed to have someone with the potential to win the world's biggest grass-court tournament. With Sampras announcing his retirement a few weeks before Wimbledon and the reigning Wimbledon champion, Lleyton Hewitt, struggling for form, the way seemed open for a new name on the Wimbledon roll of honour. The British thought they knew what that name would be – and it wasn't Roger Federer.

Andy Roddick began working with Andre Agassi's former coach Brad Gilbert after suffering a frustrating first-round defeat to Sargis Sargsian at the 2003 French Open. Like Federer, he had been the-next-big-thing-waiting-to-happen since becoming the Swiss's next-but-one successor as the world junior champion in 2000. He needed something to take him to the next level, and in Gilbert he found it.

The effect of Roddick bringing Gilbert on board was instantaneous. In their first event together, Roddick stormed through the pre-Wimbledon tournament, the Stella Artois Championships at London's Queen's Club, beating Andre Agassi in a glorious semi-final (saving a match point in doing so) and humbling Sébastien Grosjean in less than an hour to claim the title.

The British press went mad about him, nominating him as the favourite for Wimbledon, even though he was seeded fifth behind Hewitt, Agassi, Juan Carlos Ferrero and Federer. Of course, the locals still harboured hopes that Tim Henman might finally win their event, but the serious money was on Roddick. And the dramatic events of the first day hardly slowed the Roddick bandwagon.

The Centre Court programme at Wimbledon is always opened on the first day by the defending champion, and the match is normally something of a formality. Not so in 2003. For the first time since the 1966 champion Manolo Santana lost in the first round in 1967, the champion was struck down at the first hurdle, Hewitt losing in four sets to the big-serving, stammering giant from Croatia, Ivo Karlovic.

More fuel was added to the Roddick fire in the second round, when the American kept his cool while Greg Rusedski lost his. Roddick played a much more assured match than the indignant Brits were willing to acknowledge in beating Rusedski in straight sets. Rusedski led 5–2 in the third set, but then at 5–3 he let a ball go when he heard the call of 'out'. The call proved to have come from the crowd rather than the line umpire and, with his serve under threat, Rusedski went wild. With several million people watching at teatime on British terrestrial television, Rusedski let fly a tirade of expletives towards the match umpire, Lars Graff, who had been one hundred per cent correct in his application of the rules. Rusedski lost his serve and shortly after the third set, and he was the talk of Wimbledon until the following day.

Meanwhile, Federer cruised comfortably through his first couple of matches, beating Hyung Taik-Lee and Stefan Koubek each in straight sets, and then in his third match he beat Mardy Fish in four. Although no one could have guessed at the time, the thirtieth-ranked Fish was to be the only person to win a set against Federer in the whole tournament. But, after three rounds, nothing had been proved – yet. After all, Federer had never been beyond the quarter-finals, and his next opponent was Feliciano López, a Spaniard with a passion for fast courts who had reached the fourth round the previous year and whose big left-handed serve was particularly effective on grass. Yet, with Hewitt gone and Agassi, Henman, Nalbandian and Ferrero all in the bottom half of the draw, anticipation about the semi-final was growing.

A personal recollection perhaps illustrates this sense of anticipation. Over the middle weekend of that year's tournament, London's oldest Sunday newspaper, the *Observer*, asked me to write a preview of the likely semi-final between Roddick and Federer. The brief I was given was 'to look at the two players' strengths and weaknesses, explain why it should be a great match, and why Roddick should win'. 'But I don't think he *will* win,' I replied. I was allowed to make my case for Federer, although this was very much against the tide of opinion in the British media.

Fifteen minutes into Federer's match against López, the prospect of a Roddick–Federer semi-final was receding rapidly. On a cold, overcast June Monday, the two players walked out on to Court 3, the Wimbledon showcourt with fewest seats. After the first game, Federer called for the trainer, and after three he took an injury timeout. His back had seized up. 'I felt a twinge in my upper back,' he said later. 'I told the trainer what I was feeling and he massaged it but couldn't tell me what it was, so I just went on playing.'

To this day, Federer doesn't know what went wrong with his back that day. The fact that he had no further problems with it, either during that Wimbledon week or at any time since, suggests it was the nerves getting to him. Was the perennial prodigy about to flop again and fuel the growing suspicion that he was a little flaky in the big tournaments?

No, he wasn't. In fact, the injury may have been the best thing that happened to him. Fearing he might have to retire, he relaxed, and while he trailed for most of the set, a run of López errors helped Federer to break back to level at 5–5. Once he had taken the first set on a 7–5 tiebreak, he was never in trouble again.

That day, Roddick dropped his first set of the tournament, beating Paradorn Srichaphan in four and adding to the aura of the seemingly phenomenal effect Gilbert was having on Roddick's game. Nine matches the two had had together: nine wins, just three sets dropped.

Another man on a run of nine successive victories was Sjeng Schalken. The Dutchman had won the pre-Wimbledon grass-court tournament in 's-Hertogenbosch, and must have hoped Federer's back problem would help redress the balance from when the pair had played in Arnhem earlier that year, a match Federer had won in straight sets. But a break in each set sufficed for Federer to sail through. With Roddick beating the veteran Jonas Björkman, also in straight sets, the match all the neutrals wanted to see had been secured. Having a Roddick–Federer semi-final was also some minor comfort for the home fans, who that day had to endure another Tim Henman defeat, this time in the quarter-finals to Sébastien Grosjean.

If the hype surrounding the Roddick–Federer match had turned the semi-final into a spectacle that threatened to eclipse the final, it wasn't a sentiment shared by Federer. 'I expected to win it,' he says today. 'It was just the media that was hyping up everything, that he was the big favourite to win the tournament. I – how shall I say this? – I wasn't of the same opinion. Because he won Queen's and I won Halle, and because Queen's is in England, everybody was talking about him more, for about a month. But I knew that if I played my game correctly I should beat him.'

The word 'correctly' doesn't seem sufficient to describe one of the most emphatic performances of Federer's career. Even if his passage to his first Grand Slam final wasn't as big a breakthrough for him as certain other matches had been, it was the one at which he effectively announced to the tennis world that, if he was on his game, it was virtually impossible for anyone else to beat him. Roddick's comment 'I got my butt kicked' was short and to the point, but doesn't give sufficient credit to the sublime display his opponent offered on what was America's national day. Writing in a British newspaper, Boris Becker said of

Federer's display, 'A video cassette of this should be sent to every tennis coach in the world.'

One point in particular stays in the memory: the point with which Federer reached set point in the second set. Rallying from the baseline, he came in to the net on a late decision and found himself having to play a low volley. To experienced tennis watchers, he appeared to have made a tactical error that left him stranded in no-man's land. But playing the kind of shot he would normally attempt only in the last few minutes of a practice session, when the fun and artistry takes over from the hard work, he flicked the low ball cross-court, driving it ferociously into the forehand corner of Roddick's baseline. Federer himself couldn't suppress a wry smile. Even he knew it was sheer brilliance.

'I know I played a fantastic match with fantastic points,' he says today of the 7–6, 6–3, 6–3 win that took him into his first Grand Slam final, 'but that made it all the more necessary for me to settle down in the final. I got praised like crazy for beating Andy, because people had seen him playing so well, but I'd already beaten him before. It was the final I had to get up for, and that was the real breakthrough.'

Facing Federer in the final was Mark Philippoussis, the big-serving but injury-prone Australian whose five-sets victory over Andre Agassi in the tournament's fourth round seemed to have relaunched his career. Philippoussis had two advantages over Federer: he had the bigger serve and he'd been in one previous Grand Slam final, the 1998 US Open decider, which he'd lost in four sets to his compatriot Patrick Rafter. For those reasons, he had a chance – theoretically, at least.

Federer, however, had the momentum. After beating Roddick so convincingly, he could probably have lost the final and still claimed to have exorcised his demons. But, with the wind in his sails, he wasn't going to let himself be blown off course.

In the final, he out-aced Philippoussis by 21 to 14 in notching up a 7–6, 6–2, 7–6 win that was effectively decided in the first set tiebreak. At 6–2 in the third-set tiebreak, Federer had four championship points. On the first, Philippoussis delivered a big serve: 6–3. On the second, the Australian netted a return, and Federer fell to his knees.

It was what happened in the moments after Federer became Wimbledon champion that really sold him to the British public. Tears in the moment of winning a major sporting event are nothing new, even in a country like England where men crying openly is still not something many are comfortable with. By the time Federer faced a live on-court interview that was broadcast around the world, it was assumed he had 'regained his composure', as the British like to call it. He had already answered a couple of questions from the former French Open champion Sue Barker, when he described how he was finally living one of his childhood dreams. As he uttered the words 'And now I'm here!' his voice cracked with emotion, the tears of joy flowed, and he captured the hearts of a lot more than the 13,800 people in the venerable arena that day.

'There's no rule about how you should conduct yourself in the moment when you win or when you lose,' he said the following morning. 'The only thing you mustn't do is throw your racket into the crowd and injure someone. There are people who don't smile when they win, and there are people who smile for weeks afterwards. I'm the kind of guy who lets the tears flow, and I think that goes down pretty well, especially when people see this is the realisation of my biggest dream and that it's just amazing for me. I got a lot of feedback that people in the crowd also cried and enjoyed it, and it's nice to share this with a lot of people.'

One of the photographs taken immediately after the final that frequently gets reprinted shows a fan in a Swiss shirt with tears streaming down his face. That man was Michael Purek, a member at Old Boys Basel, who had been a sparring partner of Federer's in his teenage days.

While Purek was lucky enough to watch his old mate's performance courtside, most of the rest of the Old Boys fraternity were glued to the television set in the Old Boys' cramped clubhouse. 'That was a great day at the club,' said Seppli Kacovski, the man who'd taught the Wimbledon champion to play tennis. 'I was OK at the beginning, but I got so nervous that I could hardly watch in the tiebreak, and then I got so nervous I uncorked the champagne too early. It was his first match point, and suddenly there was champagne everywhere, and then Philippoussis saved it. Everyone was laughing at me, but only for one point, because Roger then won it. We drank and cried. We sang. We toasted Roger. We were so proud.'

Lots of people were proud of Federer that night, among them Peter Carter's parents, Diana and Bob, who watched the match in the South Australian town of Nuriootpa and shed their own tears at Roger's victory. It was still less than a year after Peter's death, but Bob admitted in a television interview around this time that Federer's success had helped ease the pain of their loss. 'I feel really good about it,' he said of Federer's title. 'It's a wonderful feeling, really, because Peter had such an influence on his career, and to watch Roger play you can sort of see a little of Peter there.'

Although keen not to praise any single person's contribution to his success when he faced the media after the final, Federer was happy to acknowledge Carter's role in his moment of triumph. 'Peter was one of the most important people in my career. We would have had a big party together if he was still here. I'm sure he was watching it from somewhere.'

That night, Federer was invited for the second time to the Wimbledon champions' dinner at London's Savoy hotel, and this time he accepted. The dinner always takes place very late because all champions and finalists are invited, including those from the junior events, and some don't finish playing their finals until well into the evening. The tradition of the men's and women's singles champions having the first dance with each other has long since gone (in fact, there's no dancing at the Wimbledon champions' dinner), but both singles champions are asked to make a small speech, and the moment normally falls sometime after midnight. In his, Federer said, 'This is the first time

I've attended this event. Five years ago, when I won the junior title, I declined your invitation because the following day I was playing in Gstaad. I now realise I made a mistake. I'm really proud to be here and to have earned my membership of the All England Club. I look forward to dropping by to hit a few balls at Wimbledon just for fun. If anyone wants to hit with me, give me a ring.'

Sitting close to Federer at the dinner was Francesco Ricci Bitti, the president of the International Tennis Federation. Referring back to their on-court conversation at the Rome prize-giving ceremony eight weeks earlier, when Ricci Bitti had chided Federer for the way he had lost to Felix Mantilla, Federer looked into the Italian's eyes and said, 'You see, Mr President, I *can* win these kinds of matches. Aren't you proud of me?'

Luckily for both the media and himself, Roger Federer is a good communicator. For any tennis player who does not enjoy chatting with journalists and television crews, winning a Grand Slam singles title is a serious health hazard.

As well as the obligatory post-match press conference and interview with the host television broadcaster, there are usually at least half a dozen one-on-one interview requests, often a dozen, with everyone considering it their moral right to have at least three minutes with the new champion. And that's just for the English-speakers; for someone who has their own language, you can double the time. And for someone from Switzerland, where trilingualism is nothing special, the process can take even longer. As a result, Federer has become accustomed to allowing at least an hour and sometimes much more for his media obligations after Grand Slam quarter- and semi-finals, while, for finals, it's normally about two hours, plus time for photo-shoots with whichever trophy he's won.

After winning Wimbledon in 2003, Federer duly discharged his two hours of media responsibilities before heading back to the family house in Wimbledon he'd rented for the fortnight, where he showered, shaved and quickly changed into his dinner jacket and Swiss-red bow tie. Then he was off to the Savoy, before returning home in the small hours of the morning. After a few hours' sleep, there was another round of media appointments, starting with radio and television appearances, followed by breakfast with first the British press and then any journalist wanting to converse in French, High German and Swiss German. He could have said no and enjoyed a lie-in; indeed, many champions do just that. But this wasn't just Federer's first Grand Slam title where the novelty was something to be enjoyed, he is also someone who understands the responsibilities of promoting his sport that come with being one of its high-profile champions.

That morning, the papers had glowing accounts of Federer's success, and he continued to charm them. There was no hint of irritation, or even the tired autopilot of answering the same questions over and over. He listened to every one, thought about his answers and allowed his simple humanity to shine through. 'Life will change in some ways,' he said when asked how his victory would affect him. 'I'm more famous now, a celebrity. Before, I was just a good tennis player. I don't know how that's going to be. My star sign is Leo, and Leos like to be the centre of attention, but I'll do the same work on court because, if you don't work, people will catch you.'

A bit of context is needed here. At the time that Federer won his first Wimbledon, the ATP was publicly fighting the four Grand Slam tournaments for a share of their profits. In addition, a list of tennis grandees was calling for the permissible dimensions of rackets to be reduced because, they said, tennis was getting 'tedious'. And the previous August, Lleyton Hewitt became embroiled in a dispute with the ATP that seemed to sum up tennis's problems.

At the time the undisputed world number one, Hewitt was asked to do an interview with an American television station. Both the station and the ATP had been chasing him on the matter for some time, and at the Cincinnati Masters the patience of both the ATP's communications managers and Hewitt himself boiled over. Astonishing as it might seem, the matter escalated to such a degree that the Australian took out a $1.5 million lawsuit against the organising body of the men's professional tennis tour. Irrespective of the arguments on both sides, the case seemed a metaphor for an epidemic of ills at the top of world tennis.

Into this tense environment steps a striking twenty-one-year-old man, a man of open emotions, considerable decency and the ability to express himself with great eloquence in three languages. And he wins the most prestigious prize in tennis! Federer was the kind of ambassador tennis could only dream of; the PR folk couldn't have staged it better. No wonder the sport felt good at that Wimbledon champions' dinner.

The message Federer was giving out was summed up in one sentence from his post-match press conference: 'There was big pressure from all sides, also from myself. I've proved myself to everybody. It's a big relief.' Now the real part of his career could begin.

It began with a flight on a private jet from London to Saanen, a tiny airfield high in the Swiss Alps and a few kilometres from arguably the most picturesque venue on the tennis tour: the small town of Gstaad, set amid the stunning splendour of the Bernese Oberland. The small club that hosts the tournament builds plenty of temporary seating for its week in the spotlight, but breathtaking vistas of chocolate-box scenery are always in the players' and spectators' peripheral vision, as is the fairytale castle towering over the town that looks like a drawing from a children's storybook. Gstaad is home (or second home) to many big names of the stage and screen, as well as sport (including the twelve-times Grand Slam champion Roy Emerson) and other celebrity walks of life, and the tournament would feature more prominently on the tennis map if it didn't have the graveyard slot the week after Wimbledon. Because of this unfortunate timing, it generally attracts only the hardened clay-courters for whom Wimbledon is an interruption – albeit a lucrative one – from the European red-clay season.

But in 2003 and 2004, Gstaad had the Wimbledon

champion, an almost unheard-of occurrence. And it has the legacy of a decision taken back in 1998 to thank for that.

All tournament directors like to look for promising youngsters, on the basis that promising youngsters are looking for tournament opportunities, so, if a tournament director offers a player a chance to play while the player is on the way up, that same player might look favourably on the tournament when he or she is at the top.

In 1998, the Gstaad tournament director Köbi Hermenjat had offered Switzerland's promising junior Roger Federer his first-ever match at ATP tour level and, although Roger had lost in straight sets in the first round to the Argentinian doubles specialist Lucas Arnold, he never forgot the gesture of assistance. So, instead of feeling an imaginary twinge of pain in his left calf which might have emerged during the second and third sets of the Wimbledon final and thus forced him to withdraw from a tournament which made no sense from a tennis or physical point of view, Federer honoured his commitment to Gstaad and showed up. He might also have been forgiven for tanking his first or second match, knowing that he would have turned out for the fans and could always say the tiredness from Wimbledon or his becoming reaccustomed to clay had been his undoing. But Federer isn't like that. The verb 'to tank' is barely in his vocabulary, and it's certainly not in his mentality; if he's out on a tennis court, he plays to win. Besides, he had given his word to Hermenjat that he would be there, and anyway this was the chance to celebrate. He knew his countryfolk wanted to see him, and he was determined to oblige them.

There was always going to be some sort of token present in Gstaad for the returning hero, but what a present the tournament in Gstaad hit on! After Federer's opening-round win over Marc López in three sets, his gift was brought on to the centre court. Her name was Juliette, and she was a tan-and-white Bernese Oberländer milk cow weighing something close to 800kg. She was presented to Federer decked out in a garland of sunflowers and wearing a traditional Swiss cowbell.

For a while on court, Federer looked nonplussed, but then he entered into the spirit of the gesture. Asked later by the media where he would keep her, he questioned whether she would really be happy either touring with him around the world or watching the trams go by in the streets of Basel, so he agreed to leave her to graze on the slopes of the Oberland mountains. She clearly did more than grazing; when asked at Wimbledon the following year how she was, Federer replied, 'She's doing well, and she has a calf now.'

As for the tournament at Gstaad, it was almost a phenomenal victory to follow Federer's heroics at Wimbledon. He beat the quality clay-courter Gaston Gaudio in the semi-finals in straight sets, before losing a five-set final to Jiri Novak, a Czech whose best year was the one before and whose star was beginning to fade. There would have been yodelling in the streets of Gstaad that night if Federer had won, but he'd still performed heroically; after his efforts at Wimbledon, he had not only shown up but had played all matches asked of him and fought to the end. 'I really wanted to win this for you,' he told the crowd after the final, 'because the way you have received me here has touched me greatly.'

After giving his all at Wimbledon and Gstaad, Federer admitted to being 'dead on my feet'. It was almost time for a holiday, but there was one more obligation.

Six months earlier, back in January 2003, his old friend and flatmate Yves Allegro had asked Federer if he would come to his home town of Grône, near Sion, to put in an appearance as part of the Grône tennis club's twenty-fifth anniversary celebrations. Federer had agreed to appear, telling Allegro in March that the evening of Tuesday, 15 July would be the best time to appear. 'Gstaad finishes on the Sunday, we're off on holiday on Wednesday, so we'll fit it in on Tuesday,' he had said.

When Federer won Wimbledon, the folks at Grône thought he'd now be too big to spare an evening to play a set at their club. And when he got to the final in Gstaad, they all but gave up hope. Only one person was sure Federer would show, and that was Allegro. 'I know Roger,' he says today, 'and I knew that, once he'd said he'd come, he would come unless there was really something unavoidable that would prevent it. Everyone at the club was convinced he would cancel, but I knew he wouldn't.'

Federer did indeed show up at Grône as promised and provided a memorable night for the townspeople, playing three sets against Allegro, signing autographs and posing for the camera – all without even the mention of a fee. And he saw at first hand how much it means to people to have him around.

The following morning, it was off to Sardinia for a hard-earned holiday, but off court the sweet smell of success took a different form.

In the months after she became his girlfriend, Mirka Vavrinec persuaded Federer to launch his own range of cosmetics. Ever open to new ideas, Federer agreed, and the resulting RF cosmetics line became Vavrinec's project. She developed the logo, which features Federer's autograph, and worked on the development of the range's four products: eau de toilette spray, aftershave balm, body wash and deodorant stick, plus special sets – all made in Switzerland and marketed under the slogan 'Feel the touch'. The advertising blurb describes the range as 'fulfilling the highest demands of modern sports-oriented men'.

'It's something we've done all ourselves,' said Federer proudly in an interview with the tennis-x.com website. 'It's the Roger Federer fragrance. I helped a lot with it, including the selection and refinement of the fragrances. It's something that means a lot to me. We'll see what happens.'

One can only hope Federer wasn't involved in drafting the RF advertising literature, which in places puts the most pseudo of art critics and wine writers in the shade. The eau de toilette spray, with its 'elegantly sporty fragrance', is described as having 'citrus chords and ozone elements... with a hint of green tea'. The blurb goes on: 'Transparent floral themes, noble woody notes and sensuous ambergris tones create a lingering background to round off an unmistakable, sophisticated fragrance image.' The unmistakable, sophisticated fragrance image is available only in Switzerland, although the products can be bought internationally via the internet.

Another significant off-court development in the weeks after Wimbledon was Federer's declaration of independence from his former management, a decision that fits perfectly with his sense of self-determination.

Most tennis players – indeed, most top athletes – are 'managed' by a player agency. The majority of tennis players are with one of three companies: the International Management Group (IMG), set up by the pioneering Mark McCormack in the 1960s when he turned Arnold Palmer from a successful golfer into a highly lucrative brand; Octagon Worldwide (formerly Advantage International); and SFX (formerly Pro-Serv).

Since 1998, Federer had been with IMG, but by mid-2003 he had come to the conclusion that he wanted control of his affairs closer to home, so he ended his relationship with IMG and set up Roger Federer Management. Federer himself and the people close to him were in a better position than many on the tennis circuit to take matters into their own hands. And take them they did.

Roger Federer Management had a number of high-profile officers, notably Mirka Vavrinec as Roger's diary secretary and Lynette Federer, Roger's mother, as a secretary for bigger projects. The Basel lawyer Bernhard Christen had a prominent position, and even Federer's coach Peter Lundgren was part of the team. The company was based in the offices of the law firm that Christen worked at in Bottmingen (the same suburb of Basel to which Lynette and Robbie Federer had relocated), while publicity was handled by a communications firm in Germany. Chairman and chief executive was, and remains, Roger Federer – and anyone assuming this is nothing more than a figurehead position misunderstands him; he might be willing to listen to advice, but he makes his own decisions.

Many people criticised the arrangement, notably those from other player-management companies who saw it as setting a precedent that didn't augur well for their own credibility. But Federer's entrepreneurism wasn't a unilateral declaration of independence; other players – notably the Spanish players Albert Costa and Alex Corretja – had also split from recognised agencies and put their management trust in friends and family. The critics no doubt saw themselves vindicated when, two years later, Federer went back to IMG for partial representation (IMG now looks after Federer's international marketing), but this apparent back-pedalling merely reflected the evolution of a model that clearly works for Federer and his family – Roger Federer Management decided it wanted to make more of an international brand of Roger Federer, so it enlisted the help it felt it needed. Some sceptics also suggested there was a risk that in-house management would take up too much of Federer's time and distract him from tennis. Not only have his results dismissed this fear comprehensively, but the risk of being distracted from his tennis probably stems more from the generous way in which he gives his time to the media and outside initiatives than from any internal management issues.

The Wimbledon honeymoon lasted into August, when Andy Roddick beat Federer in the semi-finals in Montreal on a final-set tiebreak. Had Federer won that match, he would have gone to the top of the rankings, but somehow he didn't seem ready for it and the result didn't feel altogether wrong. After all, Roddick was on the best roll of his career, one that would see him take the US Open and finish the year ranked number one. Nonetheless, Federer still had a match point, and the match is Roddick's only win to date against his Swiss rival.

Despite a second-round defeat to David Nalbandian in Cincinnati, Federer's Wimbledon honeymoon could be said to have lasted until the US Open, but it was there that it certainly ended. In fact, the next two months were to prove particularly troublesome for the young Swiss.

Although no one had done the Wimbledon and US Open double since Pete Sampras in 1995, Federer looked a reasonable bet to do so at a tournament without any obvious favourite. But, as the weather worsened, Nalbandian again showed up to spoil the party.

Federer cruised through his first three rounds without dropping a set, but then had to sit by as fine drizzle held up play for three days. Although only in its seventh year in the 'new' Arthur Ashe Stadium, the US Tennis Association had apparently not foreseen the problem of mild drizzle affecting the playing surface. The dark-green concrete court was fine, but at the slightest hint of moisture the white lines became as slippery as ice and play had to stop. The skies were grey for three solid days during that year's US Open and, while play seemed always on the point of starting, it never really did.

On the fourth day, the skies were still grey, but it was finally dry, and Federer took to the Arthur Ashe Stadium against Nalbandian for a place in the quarter-finals. He won the first set, but, once he'd lost the second on a tiebreak, his face took on the colour of the sky, and after that there was no way back. Asked after his 3–6, 7–6, 6–4, 6–3 defeat why he hadn't managed to beat the Argentinian in five previous meetings, Federer replied, 'I've never had a great day playing against him. I guess I'm struggling against him. I don't know how to comment on this. I'm trying to figure out how to beat him. He likes my game; that's all I can say about it.'

Nalbandian was no more illuminating, 'I like playing against him,' he said. 'What more can I say? I like his game. I don't know exactly why, but I think I know him.'

If Federer's defeat in New York against Nalbandian was demoralising, another was to follow against another nemesis in another Grand Slam arena that was more demoralising, more dramatic, and certainly more emotional.

In the aftermath of Peter Carter's death, the Swiss and Australian tennis associations had taken up a suggestion made by Australia's captain John Fitzgerald that, when the two nations met each other in the Davis Cup, they would play for the Peter Carter Trophy. Fitzgerald had a personal interest, having known Carter from their time together as boys at Peter Smith's set-up in Adelaide. The first opportunity to play for the new trophy came in September 2003, when Australia hosted Switzerland in the semi-finals. Tennis Australia chose to stage the tie in the Rod Laver Arena, the main stadium of the Australian Open's venue at Melbourne Park, and, with the previous two Wimbledon champions spearheading their teams, the stage was set for a cracker of a tie.

At that time, however, there were large question marks hanging over both teams. Federer came to Melbourne as Wimbledon champion but had made no obvious progress since Wimbledon. Switzerland welcomed back Michel Kratochvil as its second player, but he was woefully short of match practice. The same could also be said of Australia's number two, Mark Philippoussis, and even their number one, Lleyton Hewitt, hardly came into the tie with the best of records; he'd lost his Wimbledon title on the first day to Ivo Karlovic, he'd lost in the quarter-finals of the US Open to Juan Carlos Ferrero, he'd lost his number-one ranking, he'd lost his coach, Jason Stoltenberg (and people weren't at that stage sure whether his replacement, Roger Rasheed, was a mate standing in or a genuine coach – he's since proved to be the latter), and there was speculation about whether he was spending too much time with his girlfriend, Kim Clijsters, rather than concentrating on his tennis. It meant that all five rubbers of the semi-final seemed up for grabs.

With rain causing the roof to be closed for all the opening day, Hewitt crushed a disappointing Kratochvil 6–4, 6–4, 6–1. Then, in the second singles match, Federer and Philippoussis faced each other for the first time since their Wimbledon final eleven weeks earlier. The Australian claimed to have learned a lesson from the Wimbledon final, but what it was nobody could quite work out as Federer won 6–3, 6–4, 7–6(3). Philippoussis had led 5–3 in the third set, but that had been his only period of hope.

With the opening singles matches split, the doubles assumed massive importance, and it turned into what the Australian journalist Craig Gabriel described as 'a fiesta of enthralling tennis'. Since the retirement of Mark Woodforde in 2000, Australia had struggled to find a doubles pairing that did justice to the country's tradition of producing great doubles teams; the best option seemed to be Todd Woodbridge and Wayne Arthurs, but they had never looked totally convincing. So, when they faced Federer and Marc Rosset, it seemed a genuinely fifty-fifty match, and indeed it went the full distance. Unfortunately for the Swiss, that was the day Woodbridge and Arthurs played their best match together for Australia, sneaking a 4–6, 7–6, 5–7, 6–4, 6–4 win in a magnificent spectacle.

The pressure was then on Federer in the first reverse singles against Hewitt. When he won the first set 7–5, Federer equalled John McEnroe's record of thirty successive sets won in Davis Cup singles rubbers. When he won the second 6–2, he beat it. When he led Hewitt by two sets and 5–3 in the third, it seemed the formbook was holding firm and a live fifth rubber was imminent. But two things remained in Hewitt's favour: he had a good record against Federer (he'd won six of their eight matches as professionals) and he becomes even more passionate than normal when playing for his country. This is the man who, when his clothing company (the same as Federer's) refused him permission to put the name of his country on the back of his shirts and wouldn't give him any in Australia's colours, got up early one morning to dye some white shirts yellow and some white shorts green. He is a patriotic Australian to the core, and that day he showed it.

The British tennis journalist Neil Harman described the match as 'the indomitable will against the extravagant talent'. On the point of victory for the talent, the will took over. Federer was within two points of levelling the tie, but Hewitt was determined not to be beaten in front of his own people and, when Federer gave him a couple of cheap points, the tide turned. After Hewitt had taken the third-set tiebreak 7–4, Federer took a breather; it's called a 'bathroom break', and no doubt there was a genuine call of nature, but he was clearly hoping to take the opportunity to regroup. He did for a while, but it didn't last. At 5–6 in the fourth set, he served a double fault to give Hewitt a set point. Hewitt then lunged at a volley to claim the set, and with it effectively break Federer's spirit. The final score read 5–7, 2–6, 7–6, 7–5, 6–1, and Hewitt enjoyed one of the biggest adrenaline rushes of his life. 'You can take your Wimbledons and your US Opens,' he said in an on-court interview. 'This means more to me than anything.'

At the end of the tie, Federer was in tears as the Peter Carter Trophy was presented to Australia's captain, John Fitzgerald. He knew his great run in Davis Cup singles would one day come to an end, but for it to do so in the crucial rubber of the tie for the trophy named after his mentor was hard. He restated his wish to have another go in 2004, but maybe something of the romance of the Davis Cup died for Federer that day. Although he turned out for Switzerland the following year, since the 2004 quarter-final he hasn't seemed to have quite the passion for the team competition that he once had, and these days he says somewhat half-heartedly, 'I'll play Davis Cup when it fits in with the rest of my schedule.'

The dignified Fitzgerald was obviously trying to be consoling when he said after the Hewitt–Federer match, 'They're going to have some battles over the years and, goodness, what a talent Roger is! What he can do with the ball – it's like a magic wand in his hand.'

At his next tournament, in Vienna, Federer won his tenth title, and then went on to reach the semi-finals of the Madrid Masters, although in both cases didn't have to face any of his jinx players. And he also started to look tired. His sixth assault on Basel ended with defeat to Ivan Ljubicic in the second round, and he only went to Paris-Bercy because it was a Masters Series tournament. There, he scraped through a final-set tiebreak against Martin Verkerk and then lost in the quarter-finals to Tim Henman. Although Henman was enjoying the best week of his career, Federer felt at the end of his strength. His defeat by Henman, coupled with Roddick's advance to the semi-finals, made it virtually impossible for him to finish 2003 at the top of the tree, and his year seemed as good as over. He talked about not wanting to play the year-ending Tennis Masters Cup, which that year moved to Houston, and he left observers in Paris in some doubt as to whether he would even make the trip to Texas.

He probably always intended to go, and after the event he was more than glad he did. The trip provided another breakthrough moment in his career, and the one that eventually enabled him to move from a member of the elite with a Grand Slam title to the all-conquering undisputed world number one.

The round-robin format used at the Tennis Masters Cup allows a player to lose a match and still win the tournament; Pete Sampras did it four times, and Gustavo Kuerten did it the year he went to number one in the rankings. Had Federer lost his opening match to Andre Agassi, he could still have qualified for the semi-finals, but he probably wouldn't have done. Coming through the Agassi match unlocked a door for him.

The 2003 and 2004 Tennis Masters Cups were staged more by an individual than a club or organisation. Jim McIngvale had made his fortune selling affordable home furniture, and had earned the nickname 'Mattress Mack'. A committed tennis fan, he'd become the benefactor of Houston's West Side Club and won a bid to stage the year-ending showdown there for two years.

Agassi led Federer 6–4 in the final-set tiebreak. Federer saved the first match point with a service winner, but the second was a long rally in which both men missed chances. Eventually, a Federer forehand broke the deadlock. Federer had to save a third match point at 6–7, but, when he ran out a 9–7 winner, it was to release his potential like no other victory. He had beaten one of his bogeymen – three times he had played Agassi, three times he had lost. Having snatched victory from the jaws of defeat, he was not to lose to Agassi again.

Just what a sense of release Federer gained from the Agassi victory became clear the following day, when he came face to face with another of his bogeymen, David Nalbandian. Going into the match, the head-to-head record was a staggering 5–0 for Nalbandian; in fact, Federer's only win over his Argentinian nemesis had been in the Orange Bowl junior event back in December 1998. Yet the Swiss made mincemeat of the head-to-head, allowing Nalbandian just three games in a 6–3, 6–0 victory. And, in the final round-robin match, Juan Carlos Ferrero fared scarcely better than Nalbandian, picking up just four games as Federer raced to the semi-finals with a 6–3, 6–1 win.

By the time Federer and Roddick walked out for their semi-final, Roddick had secured the year-end number-one ranking, but it looked like a miscarriage of justice when Federer won a convincing 7–6, 6–2 victory.

Then came the final, and once again Federer found himself up against Agassi. Just six days had elapsed since their meeting at the start of the tournament, but it might have been a light-year, such was the progress Federer had made. Agassi didn't play badly that day, but he failed to make any impression on Federer, the Swiss describing his 6–3, 6–0, 6–4 win as 'one of the best of my life'.

After the event, Federer talked about having found something within himself, but it was an observation by Agassi that stayed in the memory. In the on-court presentation ceremony, the American congratulated Federer on the way he'd played all that week and added, 'It's a pleasure to watch you play.'

Federer's Wimbledon triumph back in July had turned something that had until then been only a trickle into a deluge. The Federer family had been hatching the idea of establishing a charitable foundation and, when the handful of requests for money from good causes suddenly multiplied after Federer had become a Grand Slam champion, it provided the impetus the Federers needed to turn intent into action.

The result was the launch of the Roger Federer Foundation in December 2003, its trustees being Lynette, Robert and Roger Federer, the lawyer Bernhard Christen and Urs Wüthrich, a member of the Basel-Land cantonal council. The foundation's mission statement is to fund projects that benefit disadvantaged children and to promote sport for young people. There was also a wish to make the most of the family's connection with South Africa, so in June 2004 the foundation joined forces with a Swiss–South African initiative called Imbewu-Suisse, the name meaning 'seed' in the Xhosa language. Founded in 2001, Imbewu works to improve social conditions for children and young people in the New Brighton township on the edge of Port Elizabeth, one of the most impoverished areas in the country. Imbewu says its aim is 'not to awaken pity but to raise interest in people for another culture and for what is happening 10,000 kilometres down south'.

Imbewu's biggest project is a sponsorship scheme under which 100 Swiss families subsidise 100 children, while other projects include schemes aimed at improving the nutrition of over 200 children, promoting sport for young people, running voluntary work schemes and providing improved healthcare. The Roger Federer Foundation therefore agreed to fund improvements to Imbewu's infrastructure in New Brighton, including paying salaries to certain Imbewu staff, and providing funds for fifty children with which to pay for their schooling, school uniform, learning materials and two meals a day. In early 2005, the three schools attended by the children who benefit from the Foundation's money held a competition to find a motto to accompany the children through their school years. And the winner was: 'I'm tomorrow's future'.

In March 2005, Federer used his absence from the Swiss Davis Cup team to travel to New Brighton to visit the results of the funding that the foundation had provided, taking with him a consignment of T-shirts, emblazoned with 'I'M TOMORROW'S FUTURE', produced by his clothing supplier. As the Swiss journalist Freddy Widmer wrote, 'The children don't know that the young man visiting them is a world-famous sportsman. They only know that the Federer Foundation will allow them what it says on their T-shirts: a future.'

Cynics might wonder if the foundation is little more than a convenient financial arrangement. Doubtless Federer does reduce his tax liability when he contributes to the foundation, but those who know him are convinced that his primary motivation behind setting up the venture is a genuine concern to divert some of his riches to the benefit of those at the bottom of the financial ladder. At the launch of the initiative, he said, 'I chose a project in South Africa because my mother grew up there, which means that I have always had a close affinity to the country. But to me South Africa is also a shining example of a country that has overcome hatred and oppression, making it a potential source of inspiration for other crisis regions around the world. Another key factor, from my point of view, is that Imbewu will allow me to help people to help themselves by providing practical and tangible support in a highly deprived area. The vast majority of the aid will benefit children and young people directly.'

On 20 December 2003, when most people were thinking more of Christmas than tennis, Federer dropped a bombshell. The Swiss media were summoned to a hastily arranged press conference in the premises of Christen Rickli Partners, the official home of Roger Federer Management, to hear that Federer had parted company from his coach,

Peter Lundgren. Federer sat there looking grim as Bernhard Christen made the official announcement. He said the Federer team had hoped to have a news conference with Lundgren present to show that it was a mutual and amicable decision, but a rumour had leaked out and had been printed in the *Neue Zürcher Zeitung* newspaper, so the announcement had to be made now.

The split would have taken no one by surprise had it happened in the first half of 2003. At that stage, Federer's game seemed to have got stuck, and tennis observers found themselves wondering – certainly before Wimbledon – whether he needed a new coach to take him to new levels. Although highly experienced as a player and coach, Lundgren's corpulent figure never quite fitted with the image of the highest sporting aspirations and, while his laidback approach might have suited Federer away from the court, was it really the right thing for him as a player? So went the whispers on the tour.

But the decision to part company after Federer's most successful year to date – when he was Wimbledon champion, had just finished the year as Tennis Masters Cup champion, and was within striking distance of the world number one Andy Roddick – took the tennis world by surprise. In Houston four weeks earlier, he'd said he had no intention of changing coaches, and indeed Lundgren had briefed the Swiss media on how he was intending to get Federer into shape for 2004, when he hoped his charge would take over the number-one ranking. But, as Federer and Vavrinec departed for a holiday in Mauritius, Federer phoned Lundgren to say their four-year professional relationship was over.

In the news conference, Federer said he'd made the decision himself. It was the result of a long process, he said, after he'd come to the conclusion that his working relationship with Lundgren had become 'everyday' and that he needed 'new impulses'. He said he was sure that he and Lundgren would remain friends.

On the day that he and Federer parted company, Lundgren, at home in Gothenburg, declined to comment. Later, he said he felt it was a move that was always likely to happen at some stage. 'This is what happens with the kind of relationship we had,' he said in an interview shortly afterwards. 'We were so close; we did everything together. We ate together. We went out together. We even played PlayStation together. Now it's good for him to carry on with something else, and I'm happy to be doing something else.'

Several months later, when Lundgren had developed a fruitful working relationship with Marat Safin, he said Safin was easier to coach than Federer because he generally took Lundgren's advice, whereas his predecessor had listened politely but normally done his own thing anyway. While this remark might add an extra brushstroke to a picture of Federer's character, it should probably be viewed with a degree of caution, as any coach is likely to say the most positive things about the player they happen to be coaching at that moment, even if it's to the relative detriment of those they've coached in the past.

There are arguments that can justify almost any decision, but Federer had just contradicted the sporting proverb: 'Never change a winning team'. He had ended 2003 on the unexpected high of Houston that gave all his followers hope for 2004, but had suddenly parted with one of the cornerstones of his 2003 success. Moreover, he had not appointed a successor. Suddenly, Federer looked a shade vulnerable again as 2004 approached.

10

ANYONE WITH AN urge to create an obstacle course designed to test whether or not Roger Federer had dealt with his demons could hardly have done better than to present him with 2004's Australian Open. Over the previous two years, he'd been beaten in the tournament in winnable fourth-round five-set matches. And there he was in 2004, without a coach, facing a run-in that looked like producing three out of the quartet of Hewitt, Nalbandian, Roddick and Agassi in the last four rounds: three of his bogeymen plus the reigning world number one.

After the shockwaves of parting from Lundgren, the world wanted to know who was going to be in Federer's corner henceforth. Federer took full responsibility for the decision and said he was in no hurry to appoint a successor to Lundgren. 'Maybe it's good to be on my own for a bit,' he'd said before the 2004 Australian Open. 'I've been given good advice for most of my life, so maybe there's something good about looking after myself for a time.' Although no one could argue with that sentiment, nor the logic of not rushing into a new coaching arrangement, for the number-two player in the world to be without a coach was generally perceived as a weakness. At least it was at the start of the year – by the end, things looked a little different.

Federer took responsibility for something else at the start of that tournament: his relations with the Swiss media. Having opted not to play a tournament before the Australian Open, he took the opportunity to acclimatise himself to conditions in Melbourne by playing at an exhibition event held the week before the Australian Open at the Kooyong Club, the tournament's former home. There he spoke to a number of journalists, granting almost every interview request. Then, on the Saturday before the Open, he did a little more media work at Melbourne Park, before telling the media liaison people he wanted Sunday off. The following day, the majority of the Swiss press showed up and were most put out to discover that their crown jewel was doing no media that day. When it was put to Federer that the Swiss press were not happy, Federer told the International Tennis Federation's on-duty player–media liaison officer that he would deal with it himself.

And he did. At the first available opportunity, he explained to the Swiss journalists that he felt that he'd done more than his fair share of media work, told them that he really did want a day off and asked them to respect that. Barbara Travers, the ITF's head of communications, said, 'It's only the second time in the nearly twenty years I've worked with tennis players that a player has said, "Leave it to me." The other was Ivan Lendl. To me, it showed an unusual but refreshing sense of taking responsibility.'

The tournament began with Federer posting three straight-sets wins against modest opposition, but then the stakes were suddenly and theatrically raised. On 26 January, Australia's national day, he came up against Lleyton Hewitt for the first time – and on the same court – since he'd lost so dramatically to the Australian from being two sets and 5–3 up in the Davis Cup semi-final four months earlier. The two shouldn't really have met so early in a Grand Slam event, but Hewitt had deliberately stayed off the tour after the US Open until the end of the year, using the time to have a bunion removed and concentrating solely on the Davis Cup. His ranking had therefore slipped to fifteenth, and he landed in Federer's eighth of the draw. As the match started, Hewitt was quick off the blocks, winning the first set to suggest that he still had Federer's number. But then something changed.

A little luck is often needed at a crucial moment, and Federer got his luck in the sixth game when Hewitt was foot-faulted after serving an ace. It wasn't a major incident, but Hewitt is seldom called for foot-faults, and players who seldom infringe the foot-fault rule generally feel mightily aggrieved when it happens, especially when – as in this case – the serve in question would have been a winner. Had Hewitt been trailing in the match, it would probably have fuelled him with the necessary aggression to bounce back, but with everything going swimmingly for the Australian the baseline umpire's call threw him momentarily off balance, Federer seized his opportunity to break, and the match turned. And, as it turned out, the destiny of the tournament too.

From then on, Federer was unstoppable. As he closed in on victory, the night skies were lit up with the traditional Australia Day fireworks display over the Melbourne skyline, adding a theatrical audio-visual backdrop to the on-court tension. But it didn't distract the champion-in-waiting. He later admitted to being a little nervous when he served for victory, the memories of the Davis Cup semi-final coming back to pose a psychological question, and when Hewitt saved two match points there was a frisson around the Rod Laver Arena, the electrified crowds daring to hope that maybe their streetfighter was to stage another comeback. But Federer was not to be denied, and converted his third match point.

After dispatching the somewhat match-rusty Hewitt to win 4–6, 6–3, 6–0, 6–4, Federer had brushed aside one jinx player – only to be greeted by another in the next round.

In the quarter-finals, Federer found himself up against Nalbandian. At least he had one win against the Argentinian from the round-robin match in Houston, but had that been for real or did Nalbandian still hold the key to Federer's game?

Among those players who have done most damage to Federer (mainly Nalbandian, Hewitt, Henman, Agassi and Nadal), the one thing they all have in common is their use of the full width of the court. Federer tends to dominate when he's able to stay mostly within the width of the 36ft (10.97m) doubles court, but like all players he becomes somewhat less effective when driven wide by angled and heavily kicking shots. It's therefore crucial for him to assert control from the outset against such players. And against Nalbandian in that quarter-final he did so almost to perfection, surviving a lapse at the end of the third set to win 7–5, 6–4, 5–7, 6–3.

Joining Nalbandian among the quarter-final casualties was the world number one, Andy Roddick, who was beaten in five sets by the mercurial Marat Safin. The Russian was playing his first tournament after a patchy 2003 that had been seriously disrupted by a wrist injury that took a good eight months to heal. His win meant Roddick would lose the top spot after the tournament, and either Federer or Juan Carlos Ferrero would take it from him.

By a twist of fate, Ferrero and Federer were up against each other in the semi-finals. It wasn't quite a straight title eliminator – had Ferrero won, he would have had to win the final to return to the top – but it felt like one. And there was no question who the better player was. If Federer had wobbled in sight of the number-one spot against Roddick in Toronto five months earlier, there was no wobble now. He was ready to rise to the pinnacle of his profession, and he did so with a crushing 6–4, 6–1, 6–4 victory (although in fairness to Ferrero, the Spaniard was carrying an injury that restricted his movement). Irrespective of the outcome of the final, Federer would become the twenty-third man to top the world rankings since the computerised system was introduced in 1973.

Not that there was any doubt that he wanted to ascend to the throne as a newly crowned Grand Slam champion, and few gave his opponent, Safin, much of a chance in the final. He'd reached the final after four successive five-set wins over Todd Martin, James Blake, Andy Roddick and the defending champion, Andre Agassi, spending nearly twenty hours on court, and, although he said his body would recover in time for the final, it was clear that he had to get off to a good start to have any chance.

He didn't. The first set went to the tiebreak, Federer took it 7–3, and, after that, the strength drained from Safin's limbs. Just over an hour later, Federer had claimed his second major title, taking the final 7–6, 6–4, 6–2.

'It's really nice,' he said later of his success, with his typical brand of understatement. 'It just gets me all emotional inside. To win the Australian Open and become number one in the world is a dream come true.' Then, when asked if he felt himself to be the best player on the planet, he replied, 'I feel I'm maybe the most natural ball-striker. I'm not going to start praising myself, but, for me, my game feels natural. I feel like I'm living the game when I'm out there. When a guy is going to hit the ball, I know exactly the angles and the spins. I just feel I've got that figured out.'

After the triumph in Melbourne, and another night-and-morning round of fulfilling media requests, Federer faced a twenty-two-hour flight back to Switzerland at the start of a Davis Cup week in which the Swiss were playing away. That didn't leave much time for celebrations, but the city of Basel laid claim to a couple of hours of his time for a civic reception and an appearance on the balcony of the striking dark-red city hall. Then it was on to another plane bound for Bucharest to prepare for Switzerland's Davis Cup first-round tie against Romania.

Despite not being fully over his jetlag, Federer had no difficulty beating Romania's Victor Hanescu in the second singles match in Bucharest just five days after his triumph in Melbourne (less than five when you take the time difference into account). With Andrei Pavel having beaten Michel Kratochvil in the first match, Federer's real heroics came in the doubles where, teaming with his friend Yves Allegro for the first time in the Davis Cup, the Swiss beat Pavel and Gabriel Trifu 10–8 in the fifth set. It was a thrilling match, lasting three hours and thirty-six minutes and creating a great atmosphere in Bucharest's Sala Polivalenta. With Allegro very nervous on his representative debut, Federer took on more than his fair share of the load. 'Federer played on three-quarters of the court,' said Trifu after the match. 'Everywhere we tried to send the ball, it was him, even when we were looking for Allegro.'

Then, when Federer finished off Pavel in straight sets in the first of Sunday's singles matches, Switzerland were through to their third quarter-final in four years.

In the two months between the Romania tie and the quarter-final against France in early April, Federer broke another of his jinxes. When he lost to Tim Henman in the quarter-finals in Rotterdam in mid-February, he had just one win in six matches against the Briton. But the two met again three weeks later in the final of the Pacific Life Open at Indian Wells, a resort in the California Desert for the well-to-do where the balls fly slightly freakishly through the air, giving the venue a tendency for producing some unusual results. Federer won the final 6–3, 6–3 and, while the result bucked the trend of their head-to-head record, it was the end of Henman's hold over Federer, a hold he was never to regain.

The champion in Indian Wells is often the favourite to win the ensuing Masters Series event, the Nasdaq-100 Open in Miami, but in 2004 Federer was bundled out early in only his second defeat of the year. He came on court for his third-round match against the seventeen-year-old Spaniard Rafael Nadal with a cold, but the way that the youngster set about his business made everyone sit up and take note, and his 6–3, 6–3 victory was well deserved. Although Federer would later beat Nadal in the following year's final, it would be no easy task. Nadal was already proving to be a tough nut to crack.

Switzerland's 2004 home Davis Cup quarter-final against France was a chance for the Swiss to exact revenge after their defeat three years earlier in Neuchâtel, especially as the personnel were almost exactly the same as in 2001.

There was no off-court unrest within the Swiss camp, but this time Switzerland's second-best singles player was the 134th-ranked Ivo Heuberger. Once again, the home nation's chances were highly dependent on Federer winning his two singles matches and the doubles.

The reception Federer received in Lausanne's Prilly Arena when he stepped out on court to open the tie against France's Nicolas Escudé gave even the neutrals and French supporters goosebumps. The predominantly Swiss crowd – all clad in scarlet T-shirts, creating an amazing visual tableau – were treating the match as their hero's festive homecoming following his ascent to the top of the rankings in Australia. An emotional character such as Federer could have been forgiven for taking a few games to get into his tennis after such a heartfelt welcome, but his start was anything but slow. He rode the tide of emotion to win the first four games, conceding just ten in total in a highly emphatic 6–2, 6–4, 6–4 victory.

Yet Switzerland's dependence on Federer was shown up in the second singles match. Ivo Heuberger made no impression on either his opponent, Arnaud Clément, or indeed his captain, Marc Rosset. After Heuberger's 6–3, 6–2, 6–2 defeat, Rosset made it as clear as he could without being insulting that he was singularly unimpressed with Heuberger's form and suggested that the man from eastern Switzerland would play no further part in the Swiss Davis Cup set-up as long as Rosset was in charge. The suggestion also made it even clearer that Federer and

Allegro needed to win the doubles if a home victory was a realistic possibility.

Hence the delight of the French pair, Escudé and Michaël Llodra, when they won the doubles. In fact, when Llodra made an interception at the net to win the third-set tiebreak 7–5, such was his demonstrative celebration that anyone watching could have been forgiven for thinking that France had won the Davis Cup. Llodra knew that France had broken the back of the match, and so it proved, the visitors winning 6–7, 7–3, 7–6, 6–3.

Once again, Switzerland's fate was no longer solely in Federer's hands, and once again Michel Kratochvil had yet to play a live fifth rubber after Federer's 6–2, 7–5, 6–4 drubbing of Arnaud Clément. Persistent knee problems had reduced Kratochvil's ranking to 194th, and against the sixty-eighth-ranked Escudé he lacked both confidence and nerve. Although Escudé too had been off the tour for the last six months of 2003 with a hip injury, the Frenchman had too much nous for Kratochvil, and even came back from being 3–6 down in a third-set tiebreak to beat Kratochvil 7–6, 6–3, 7–6. Once again, Switzerland's reliance on Federer was just a bit too great.

At the Swiss team's post-tie press conference, Kratochvil got visibly irritated with one of Federer's off-the-cuff comments. Some of the things Federer said in interviews that day suggested his love affair with the Davis Cup was waning. 'At least I now know where I stand in terms of tournament planning for the rest of the year,' he said with some relief. 'Last year I didn't know whether I'd be needed during the off season, but now I know I won't have to play Davis Cup for another ten months.'

As it transpired, he didn't play for Switzerland again for another seventeen months, and in the intervening period the Davis Cup weekends ceased to be one of the first entries in his schedule when he and his entourage began planning his itinerary for 2005.

As one of the top earners in the world of tennis, Roger Federer has a number of business interests. As many of these are conducted in his name by advisers, they don't add too much to the overall picture of him as a person and athlete. But one such venture from 2004 does stand out as an indication of how he clearly leans towards the country of his mother's birth.

That year, Federer bought a plot of land on the Pezula private golf estate near Knysna, a resort in the Cape just north of South Africa's much-promoted Garden Route. And, when he travelled to South Africa in March 2005 to visit the Imbewu project that receives funds from the Roger Federer Foundation, he made arrangements to build a house on his plot, which could become an off-season base in years to come.

Pezula advertises itself as the place in which 'to rub shoulders with international tennis stars and local sports heroes'. Among others who have bought land there are the golfer Nick Price, the South African national cricket-team captain Graeme Smith and a handful of tennis players, including the Swedes Jonas Björkman and Thomas

Johansson. The link with tennis comes largely from the fact that Gary Muller – a former doubles specialist and ATP council member – has not only bought property there but is also in charge of what a Pezula press release describes as a '50 million-rand "Field of Dreams" multi-faceted sports facility... in a central position on the estate... [with] three tennis courts (one in a stadium), squash courts, a golf driving range, an international-standard cricket oval, a gymnasium and a swimming pool – and it will be linked into an equestrian centre and Pezula's own sailing and beach clubs'.

Yet suggestions that Federer might be building a base in South Africa on the Pezula estate seemed to be in doubt a year after his visit there. Asked in March 2006 about his plans for the plot, he replied, 'It's on hold. We'll see. I had plans, but we're waiting at the moment.' When pushed on what he was waiting for, he replied, 'Waiting to play better!' Given that he was unbeaten in 2006 and streets ahead of the rest at the top of the rankings, he was clearly enjoying the joke, but clearly the investment was not developing the way he had hoped.

After this trip, it was back to Europe, and the clay-court season. Having notched up Grand Slam titles on grass and hard courts, Federer's next challenge was for one on clay and, after two successive first-round defeats at Roland Garros, 2005 had to be different.

Federer travelled to Paris having again won one of the clay-court Masters Series tournaments in the build-up. He won Hamburg for the second time in three years, but this time it didn't make him any more of a favourite for Paris than he would have been anyway as the undisputed world number one. And, just as Luis Horna had seemed a reasonable first-round draw the previous year, no one could assume that Federer's first opponent at the 2004 French Open, Kristof Vliegen, would be easy to beat. Perhaps for that reason, the poor Belgian became cannon-fodder for Federer's first win at Roland Garros in three years, winning just four games against the rampant top seed.

Following this trouncing, a second straight-sets win over Nicolas Kiefer set up an appetising third-round clash against Gustavo Kuerten. The Brazilian, known affectionately as 'Guga', had been Paris's darling since his first shock title in 1997 when he took the tennis world by storm by winning with a ranking of 66. In 2001, his relationship with the Paris public intensified when, after winning his third title there, he chalked into the clay a heart, in the centre of which he lay flat on his back. The Roland Garros crowd, so hard to please if a player once crosses them, just adored him, and he loved them back. By 2004, however, a troubled recovery from a complicated hip operation in 2002 had taken its toll on the likeable beach boy, and it was widely assumed that time and Federer would have caught up with him. By and large, that was the case, but, as with many greats who know their best is behind them, they can still summon themselves for the odd great match, even if they're no longer capable of winning a great tournament. That's what Kuerten did in the feature match of the first Saturday.

Playing some of the tennis that saw him top the rankings for forty weeks in 2000–01, Kuerten took Federer apart, winning 6–4, 6–4, 6–4. He took Federer's first two service games, broke early in the second and third sets and, apart from one dropped service game at the beginning, he was never broken. 'It's like a love affair between me and the crowd,' he said afterwards. 'If it wasn't for this tournament, I wouldn't be here. I'm just happy I can play here, given the way my physical condition has been. Any other tournament and I'd have pulled out.'

No doubt Federer wished he had. He clearly still had something to learn about dealing with true clay-court specialists. 'I tried but he didn't give me much of a chance,' he said afterwards. 'Usually I can control these kinds of matches, but today that wasn't the case. Guga deserved to win. Now I'm just looking forward to getting out on the grass.'

Federer's second Wimbledon triumph will probably end up as one of his less memorable major wins, but it drove another stake through the confidence of his rivals.

He again warmed up by playing in Halle, defending his Gerry Weber Open title without dropping a set and cutting the entertainment to less than an hour in a clinical demolition of Mardy Fish. The American had been the only player to take a set from Federer at Wimbledon the previous year, but in Halle in 2004 he won just three games in the fifty-nine-minute match.

Then at Wimbledon, he again dropped just one set en route to the final. That was against Lleyton Hewitt in the quarter-finals, but far from being a signal that he might be beatable, Federer was so stung to have lost a set that he won the following one to love, to run out a 6–1, 6–7, 6–0, 6–4 winner. Then a win over Sébastien Grosjean in the semi-finals set him up for another match against Roddick.

With a number of Wimbledon's spectators being very much occasional tennis fans (many wonder what the players do during the forty-eight weeks of the year when the tennis circuit isn't in England), the final between Federer and Roddick was billed as a great rematch from the previous year's semi-final. It was their seventh match, and Federer had won five of the previous six, but Roddick seemed focused and determined to make the most of his one advantage over the Swiss: his sheer power. While he'd lost his number-one ranking in Australia, Roddick was still the world number two and saw himself as the principal threat to the reigning champion. And with the fastest serve in tennis, Wimbledon was the place to make it pay.

On a showery day, Roddick came out fastest. He looked the better player before rain held up play after just five games. Rain breaks can turn matches, often because they allow players to consult their coaches in the locker room, but Federer had no coach. When the players came back on court, he looked subdued, and Roddick stormed to the first set.

Roddick couldn't hold his level, though, and Federer raced to a 4–0 lead in the second set without ever looking totally convincing. He'd created such a dominating reputation for himself that the set was as good as gone, but his curious display continued as Roddick got both breaks back and levelled at 5–5. Then, with Roddick serving at 5–6, Federer profited from a lucky net cord that gave him set point and, when he then hit a running forehand down Roddick's backhand wing to level the match, he screamed and punched the air with real emotion. The real Federer, it seemed, was back.

Or was he? In the third game of the third set, it was the passive Federer who dropped his serve, and at 2–4 he was in serious trouble. Then it rained again. Roddick walked off to talk to his coach, Brad Gilbert, while Federer went off to talk to... well, himself. During that period of introspection, he worked out that he had to be a little more pro-active to counter Roddick's aggression. And, when he came back out on court, it was a different match.

When Federer took the third-set tiebreak 7–3, Roddick could have folded, but the combination of his conviction that his power would win out and Federer's inconsistent display gave the American good reason to hope. Early in the fourth set he created six break points but converted none of them. That failure proved costly, for at 3–3 Federer broke, and the game was up for the American, Federer running out a 4–6, 7–5, 7–6, 6–4 winner.

The Reuters news agency tennis writer, Ossian Shine, used a nice analogy in his report of the match. 'Certainly,' he wrote, 'there was a moral in there somewhere, one of which Aesop would have been proud, regarding the Swiss's steady, deliberate progress overcoming Roddick's whizzbang fireworks and general uproar.'

'I got lucky, for sure,' was Federer's more modest verdict. 'I was down a break in the third set, and if Andy had served a few better games it would have been two sets.'

After the match, Sue Barker came on court to conduct brief interviews with the two players. Roddick must have felt sick about having let Federer get away, but he still managed to muster enough wit to charm the British public. 'I threw the kitchen sink at him,' he said, 'but he went to the bathroom and got the tub.'

Yet it was another bit of Roddick wit which told the truer story. Barker asked Roddick about the 'great rivalry' he had with Federer, to which Roddick replied, 'I'm going to have to start winning some of these matches if we're going to call it a rivalry.' The crowd loved Roddick's humility, but his response had summed up what Federer's third Grand Slam title meant to the tennis world in general: while he had challengers, he certainly had no rivals based on equality of expectation, except perhaps on clay.

In the eyes of many tennis watchers, it's what Federer achieved over the four weeks after Wimbledon in 2004 that qualifies him for greatness. Not since Björn Borg in 1979 had a player won three successive tournaments on different surfaces, but Federer did just that.

Arriving in Gstaad the day after Wimbledon, Federer made the often difficult transition from grass to clay in a matter of hours and, six days later, Gstaad had its home-grown champion. Although the list of people Federer beat that week hardly reads like a who's who of clay-court tennis, it was still a momentous achievement when he beat

Igor Andreev in a four-set final to finally win a title on Swiss soil. Although he didn't say so at the time, he'd come to the conclusion that Gstaad's position in the tennis calendar was too impractical for him, and in early 2005 he announced it would no longer have a place in his annual tournament schedule.

A short holiday followed, before he took to the court again on the concrete of Toronto. Again, Roddick awaited him in the final, and again Roddick's weapons weren't accurate enough to stop the Swiss clock. It was Federer's nineteenth tour title and his fourth Masters Series shield – and he wasn't even twenty-three.

As he left Toronto for the next Masters Series event in Cincinnati in early August, he had lost just four matches all year, and was unbeaten in his last twenty-three. But such success can work against players, especially if they plan their tournament schedule around an average of three or four matches per week. He was getting tired, and yet he was committed to play in Cincinnati the week after Toronto. Mercifully, he lost in the first round to Dominik Hrbaty, earning him vital recuperation time, and yet his defeat was no tank; he'd stormed through the first set to win it 6–1 before losing the match 1–6, 7–6, 6–4. It was the first time he'd been defeated in the first round since losing to Luis Horna at the 2003 French Open, but it was not a day for sadness. 'I had a great run,' he said later of his twenty-three-match winning streak. 'Maybe it was one tournament too many for me, but it's ended now. I'm not disappointed. No one should feel sorry for me. I'm going to take a few days off.'

During those days off, the Federer look began to change. At first, the changes were subtle, and the complete new look wasn't unveiled until the Tennis Masters Cup in November, but after Cincinnati he had a haircut that looked as if it hadn't quite worked, for when he turned up at the Olympics in Athens his hair was held in place not just by the usual bandanna and ponytail but by a set of hairpins, too. When he was on court, his hair didn't look that different, but when he appeared without the bandanna the layering effect was somewhat unusual.

The Athens Olympics gave him the chance of an honour he was to appreciate to the full. Having put Switzerland not just on the tennis map but the general sporting map too, he was asked to carry the Swiss flag in the opening ceremony. But his bigger goal – in fact his main goal of 2004, he said – was to win an Olympic gold medal, either in singles or doubles.

His first match in Athens, a stuttering 6–3, 5–7, 6–1 win over Russia's Nikolay Davydenko, serves to emphasise that the volatile Federer hadn't disappeared; he'd merely hidden it from view, and occasionally a safety valve had to be released. Federer served for the match in the second set, but when he played a poor game and was broken he belted a loose ball on to the roof of the centre court and earned a code violation from the umpire. 'It's a long time since I got my last warning,' he said after the match. 'For me, it was a sign. I just needed to show a reaction because I was unhappy with the way I played in the second set. I got frustrated. But the important thing is that I won, not how

I acted on court.' The hidden meaning behind that assessment can be found in his analysis of the outburst in Hamburg in 2001, when he felt that by learning to control his temper he risked becoming too passive. In other words: while he'd learned to keep his composure on court, even the cool, calm and collected Roger Federer needed to vent his spleen on occasions.

He also admitted he'd have to play a lot better in his next match, against a player he had never faced before, a tall eighteen-year-old Czech, Tomas Berdych. With his mop of ginger hair, Berdych had become known on the circuit as a promising prospect but was still ranked only seventy-fourth coming into the Olympics. On a windy day, on an outside court, he was to make his introductory statement to the tennis world. Why the world number one and gold medal favourite was on an outside court is perhaps another question (then again, why shouldn't the very best also play on the lesser courts as long as their safety isn't compromised?), but it clearly added to the effect of the swirling wind. And when, after the match, Andy Roddick walked into the locker room, having saved three match points in a thriller against Tommy Haas, saw Federer and threw him the casual question, 'How'd you get on?', he was astonished to hear Federer reply, 'I lost.'

Against Berdych, Federer looked sluggish, even in taking the first set, but a single break and adequate serving proved to be enough. Then, at 3–4 in the second set, Berdych broke Federer to love. Federer broke back but then lost his next-but-one service game with a run of errors and

Berdych took the set. With the wind acting as a leveller and Berdych doing some tremendous retrieving, Federer began to lose confidence in his serve. It just about saw him through to 5–5, but he then had to save two match points at 4–5. Then, at 5–6, he hit a double fault and made three unforced errors to give Berdych the biggest win of his career, the final scoreline reading 4–6, 7–5, 7–5.

'It's hard to play these big players on centre court because they have more practice there,' said Berdych in the post-match press conference. 'It's easier on the outside courts, where they haven't been practising or playing.'

Federer didn't do his own press conference until much later. Immediately after his defeat, he sat motionless for several minutes in the locker room, not knowing how to take it in. And by the time he faced the media, he was even more demoralised, for by then he and Yves Allegro had lost 6–2, 7–6 in the doubles to the Indian pair of Mahesh Bhupathi and Leander Paes. 'It's a terrible day for me, losing singles and doubles,' he said. 'I've been playing non-stop, you know, and it's obvious it's going to catch up with me eventually. Unfortunately, it's during the Olympics.'

Hindsight is a wonderful thing, but, if Federer had known that day that it would be more than five months before his next defeat, he would probably have felt considerably better.

The US Open is more than just a tennis tournament. It reflects the city of New York, with all its brashness. As a tournament, it's a little less brash today than it was between 1978 and 1996, when the main stadium was a hurriedly rehashed version of an open-air concert venue used by the jazz musician Louis Armstrong during the World Trade Fair of 1964, but it still takes a certain mentality to get used to the environment, especially for non-Americans. In the late 1980s, when playing on the outside courts meant inhaling the aroma of barbecued spare ribs from the chaotic food court, the Swedish champion Stefan Edberg got so fazed by the atmosphere that he threatened never to return there, until his coach, Tony Pickard, suggested that he stay in a family house on Long Island to give him a little peace. (It did the trick; Edberg won the US Open twice and played his best match there in the 1991 final.) Even Jim Courier, an American who made it to number one in the rankings, suggested the site at Flushing Meadows should be 'nuked'.

Although he always professed to enjoy his trips to New York, Federer does not have the natural personality to thrive in New York conditions. And having failed to make any in-roads against Nalbandian in the 2004 US Open, there was a question mark hanging over his capacity to win the top American tournament, certainly at the age of just twenty-three. But it was in New York that he was to make one of the most emphatic statements of his career.

He didn't look totally comfortable in his second-round match against the smiling Cypriot Marcos Baghdatis, nor in his third-round outing against the wily Frenchman Fabrice Santoro, but he raised his game when he needed to and qualified for the second week. A walkover against the Romanian Andrei Pavel, who couldn't play because of a herniated disc, meant Federer could conserve a little energy for his quarter-final, in which he had to go to five sets to beat Andre Agassi in a match played in quite ridiculous wind. With much calmer conditions for his semi-final, he showed that he'd worked out how to play Tim Henman, beating the Brit for the loss of just eleven games. But those eleven games looked a massive achievement for Henman in the light of Federer's superb display in the final.

On 12 September 2004, Federer stepped out to face another old nemesis, Lleyton Hewitt. At that time, the Australian was the man of the moment, and in some people's eyes was the favourite for the Open title, having won it three years earlier. More pertinently, he'd won four titles on the 2004 North American summer hard-court swing and was clearly the form player coming into both the tournament and the final. Yet Hewitt was humbled by one of the most impressive displays of sporting prowess of modern times. Only once did Federer wobble, that was towards the end of the second set when Hewitt had a couple of chances, but, once the Swiss had taken the tiebreak 7–3, he was irresistible. The US Open – or US nationals, as it was called before 1968 – dates back to 1881, yet you had to go back to 1884 to find the last time there had been two 'bagels' (6–0 sets) in a final.

After taking out his hairpins prior to the trophy-presentation ceremony, Federer did an on-court interview with the veteran CBS sports commentator Dick Enberg, who had just commentated on the final. Enberg tried to do justice to Federer's performance by asking him, 'Roger, I don't know where to start. We're up in the television booth, raving about your forehand, then it's your backhand, and then all of a sudden you go to the net and you made all but four of thirty-two points at the net. What else do we have to look forward to in the future?'

To which Federer replied, 'That's all I've got!'

The world was on his racket strings. From America he next went to Asia, had a holiday, and then won the title in Bangkok, where he again beat Roddick in the final. And, when he flew back to Switzerland shortly afterwards, he must have been thinking that surely, this time, Basel would finally be his.

In the first round of the Swiss Indoors, Federer was scheduled to play Luis Horna, the last man to beat him before he'd become a Grand Slam champion. They were scheduled to play each other for the first time since that frustrating day in Paris, but on the Monday afternoon of the week of the tournament, he began to feel a twinge in his thigh. By the following day, it had become clear he'd torn a muscle and was forced to withdraw. In doing so, he had to wave goodbye not only to the Swiss Indoors tournament but also to the final Masters Series event in Paris as well.

Federer's absence from the last couple of weeks of the 2004 ATP circuit meant there was something of a question mark hanging over his participation at the Tennis Masters Cup. He duly flew to Houston, sporting the post-ponytail look for the first time, but as he took to the court of the

West Side Club, a year after his breakthrough win there over Agassi, many felt that he might be vulnerable after his injury lay-off. Such feelings lasted about ten minutes into his first match against the shock French Open champion Gaston Gaudio. He took Gaudio apart in the first set and, while the Argentinian came back in the second, Federer still ran out a 6–1, 7–6 winner.

Although the cream of the tennis world was gathered in Houston, Federer no longer feared any of his rivals. 'I respect everybody but fear nobody,' was his stated philosophy.

His former bogeyman Lleyton Hewitt was dispatched 6–3, 6–3 in the next round-robin match, and even the Spaniard Carlos Moya – who was in good form and getting his playing level up for the Davis Cup final he was due to contest at home to the USA two weeks later – could do no more than take a set from the world number one.

But then in the semi-finals came one of those moments of theatre that make all the run-of-the-mill 6–1, 6–2 early-round scorelines worth tolerating. Federer's match against Marat Safin was always going to have a poignancy about it, because since May Safin had been working with Federer's former coach, Peter Lundgren. Here were the two players facing each other for the first time since Safin began working with Lundgren, and at the tournament that, a year earlier, had been the last in the Federer–Lundgren partnership.

There was just one break of serve in the whole match, and that allowed Federer to take the first set. But the key statistic was the tiebreak score with which he took the second set in his 6–3, 7–6 win: 20–18. The tiebreak lasted twenty-six minutes. Safin saved seven match points, Federer saved six set points – and the tennis was outstanding, pure drama. And when Federer converted his eighth match point to move through to the final, the two men had equalled the record for the longest ever tiebreak (measured in points) set by Goran Ivanisevic and Daniel Nestor at the US Open eleven years earlier.

After such a match, Federer might have been mentally exhausted, but he did an hour and a half's media work, accepting every interview request handed in. Admirable though that is, such generosity of time and spirit has created a rod for his own back, to the point where most reporters and broadcasters now feel unfairly rebuffed if he refuses them an interview. Quite rightly, he sees his dealings with the media as part of his duty to the sport that has nourished his bank account so well, but, as he's subsequently learned, even the generous Roger Federer has to say no on occasions.

After such drama, the final couldn't hope to live up to the same standards – and it didn't. This was through no fault of Federer and Hewitt, who were facing each other for the sixth time that year and the third time in nine weeks. Heavy rain reduced the match to a best-of-three-sets contest (and ensured that the ATP and ITF will never award it to an outdoor venue again), and the rain meant it was played late at night, by which time many television stations had cancelled their coverage. Although Hewitt battled bravely, the match served only to show what the previous two had done: that, when Federer is on his game, Hewitt doesn't have a chance against him.

So ended a year in which Federer had become the first man since Mats Wilander sixteen years earlier to win three of the four major titles in the same year (although, in fairness, Pete Sampras held three of the four titles for much of 1994 but had won them across two calendar years). He'd won seventy-four of the eighty matches he'd contested, a ratio not seen since Ivan Lendl's most consistent year of 1986. He was clearly the tennis player of the year, but he was more than that. The World Sports Academy awarded him its Laureus Award as the 2004 world sportsman of the year, arguably the most prestigious honour in world sport.

And all without a coach.

11

AFTER DOING SO well in 2004, it would have been no disgrace for Federer to have had a slightly less lustrous 2005. But no. If anything, he would scale even greater heights in 2005, certainly in terms of consistency.

He set out his stall before hitting his first ball of the new year by hiring the former Australian great Tony Roche as his part-time coach. Born in Wagga-Wagga, the wily but somewhat inscrutable Roche, a former French Open champion and thirteen-times Grand Slam doubles winner, made his name as a coach in the 1980s with Ivan Lendl. He'd taken on the task after Lendl had had a succession of coaches who'd failed to lead him to Grand Slam success, despite his immense potential. Had Federer signed up Roche in the first half of 2003, the circumstances would have been almost identical to those in which Roche began working with Lendl. In the 1990s, the Australian had worked as a casual coach to Patrick Rafter, escorting him to two US Open titles and a week at the top of the rankings. And he was also Australia's Davis Cup coach, under the captaincy of his former doubles partner John Newcombe, which allowed him to play a leading role in the development of the young Lleyton Hewitt.

Federer had first approached Roche in February 2004. The Australian – then fifty-eight and increasingly reluctant to travel both for personal reasons and because of a hip problem – turned him down, but did travel with Federer on two occasions. In mid-December 2004, Federer flew to Sydney, ostensibly to acclimatise for the Australian Open, but, as he was playing the Qatar Open in the first week of January, the trip had a different justification. He went to Roche's home to discuss the Australian becoming his coach. Roche again said he didn't want to do much travelling, so Federer worked out a part-time deal that would commit the Aussie to just ten weeks' travelling per year.

On 5 January, after beating David Ferrer in the first round in Doha, Qatar, Federer told the media of his new signing. 'It's good to know that there is help there, because I need someone to analyse and help improve my game.'

When the news was reported in Australia, the former doubles champion turned television pundit John Alexander said, 'It's a great shame for Australian tennis.' Alexander's comment reflected not only the esteem in which Roche was held down under, but also the fact that one of Australia's top coaches was working not with Australia's top player Hewitt, but with Hewitt's principal rival.

Federer went on to win in Doha, beating Ivan Ljubicic in the final, and then it was on to the Australian Open in Melbourne, where he teamed up with Roche for the first time since their new working relationship had been announced. There, playing what seemed effortless tennis, Federer breezed through to the quarter-finals for an eagerly awaited clash with Andre Agassi.

Although the American was fast approaching his thirty-fifth birthday, Agassi was still a factor in Australia, having won the title on four previous occasions, most recently in 2003, and had only lost in 2004 in a five-set semi-final to Marat Safin. If there was anywhere Agassi still had a chance against Federer, it seemed to be on the high-bouncing Rebound Ace courts of Melbourne. The theory might well have been valid, but on a balmy late summer's evening Federer won before the last of the daylight had disappeared, notching up a 6–3, 6–4, 6–4 victory over the popular American in what is likely to prove Agassi's last-ever match on the Rod Laver Arena.

But he picked up an injury in the course of the win. He said nothing about it afterwards, but it was to hamper him in his eagerly awaited semi-final against Safin, their first match since the epic 20–18 tiebreak from Houston two months earlier.

The tournament had already been blessed with four matches of the kind of quality and drama that most tournaments would normally be glad to have one of – Hewitt–Nadal, Molik–Davenport, Hewitt–Nalbandian and Serena Williams–Sharapova – so drama was in the air when Federer and Safin entered the arena on the Russian's twenty-fifth birthday. The first of the men's semi-finals was a mouth-watering prospect, and the reality lived up to the promise.

When tennis watchers are asked for a list of their all-time most memorable matches, their responses are obviously many and varied. A truly great match normally has an off-court element alongside the actual tennis, like Jimmy Connors suing the ATP's president Arthur Ashe at the time the two met in the Wimbledon final of 1975, or Pete Sampras learning that his coach Tim Gullikson had an inoperable brain tumour just before his five-sets quarter-final against Jim Courier at the 1995 Australian Open (a match in which Sampras played – and won – the final set with tears streaming down his face). If an extra-tennis element is a criterion for greatness, then the Federer–Safin semi-final of 2005 falls slightly short of the all-time great category, but it was nevertheless the most enthralling and entertaining match of the 2005 tennis year.

What had most people on the edge of their seats was the fact that Federer was clearly unsettled in the early stages of the match. Although hardly as volatile as he had been in his junior days, he was growling about the court as Safin matched him shot for shot. He won the first set, but then Safin came back to level. Federer won the third set 7–5 – the same score with which he'd won the first – and when the fourth set came to a tiebreak he looked set to edge through to what would have been the first leg of a dream final for the organisers. For waiting in the wings was

Lleyton Hewitt, who was all set to become the first Aussie finalist at the Australian Open in seventeen years if he beat Andy Roddick in the semi-final the next day – which he did. In the centenary Australian Open, marketed under the banner '100 years in the making', the semi-final line-up offered the prospect of a home player contesting the final against the defending champion and world number one.

Back in the fourth-set tiebreak of the Federer–Safin match, neither player ever had a significant lead, but then Federer got to match point at 6–5. A baseline rally developed, then Federer went to the net, Safin tried to pass him on his backhand side and Federer stretched for an exquisite backhand volley that just cleared the net. Surely that was good enough to win the point? But no. Safin raced forward and got the ball back. Federer played a second volley at Safin. Safin played the only shot he could: a lob. Federer chased it back. He seemed to have the option of playing a high defensive lob or an audacious attempted pass – either would have made sense. Instead, the controlled, disciplined Federer – the man who'd supposedly put his junior tricks behind him – had a rush of blood and attempted a 'hot dog', the flamboyant but highly risky shot through the legs with the player's back to the net. It failed, and Safin levelled the tiebreak at 6–6. It was to prove Federer's only match point.

When asked after the match what he'd thought he was doing playing a shot like that, he seemed slightly nonplussed by the question. 'Well, the point was already lost, so I tried it,' he said. Maybe he believed it at the time, but more likely he felt very silly about choosing such an ambitious shot at such a crucial stage of the match and just wanted to keep the attention away from it. There are plenty of tennis watchers who would love to see Federer attempt a hot dog and a few other showy shots, but they would expect it in the early part of an early set, not at match point in the fourth-set tiebreak of a Grand Slam semi-final!

Being Federer, he might still have won the match, but from that point on the momentum changed. Safin won the next two points to take the match into a fifth set, at which point Federer called for the physiotherapist. The trapped nerve he'd sustained during his match against Agassi was sending pain right down his playing arm. The match, it seemed, was now Safin's.

It seemed even more Safin's when the Russian opened up a 5–2 lead in the fifth set. Federer was obviously in great pain but hanging in there. He saved a handful of match points, broke back in the ninth game and hauled the set level at 5–5. Then, at 6–6, with Safin serving, Federer led 0–30, but the Russian snuffed out the danger.

Because he was serving second, Federer was always under more pressure than his opponent, and at 7–8, it showed. Safin worked his way to match point – his seventh in total. Federer couldn't gain an advantage with his serve, Safin hit a big backhand and Federer lunged for the ball, got it back but dropped his racket in the process. The court was then open for Safin, who might have been put off by Federer's loose racket, but he wasn't – his volley crashed into an unguarded court with Federer stranded. Thus, the Russian claimed the second-greatest victory of his career after his win over Pete Sampras in the 2000 US Open final.

The match had lasted four hours and twenty-eight minutes and was another triumph for the Australian Open in its centenary year. It was also a considerable triumph for Peter Lundgren, who had coached his charge to a win over the man he'd helped to make pretty much unbeatable in the first place. Little wonder the Swede was mildly tearful at the end.

When asked after the match about the injury that had proved to be his undoing, Federer was philosophical. 'It's always going to hurt, no matter how great the match was,' he admitted, 'but at least I can leave the place feeling good about myself, because I gave it all I had.'

Despite losing to Safin, the way in which he lost hardly made Federer appear vulnerable to the rest of the tennis world. His twenty-seven-match winning streak – dating back to the Berdych defeat at the Olympics – may have been broken, but Safin had played to his full potential and still needed a Federer aberration to stave off match point. Federer was still the man to beat, and he was to prove it decisively over the next two months.

His next two tournaments provided finals against Ivan Ljubicic, the late-developing Croatian who finally came good in 2005, breaking into the world's top ten after reaching eight finals, winning two of them, and steering Croatia to its first Davis Cup title. He might have won more than his two finals if three of the six that got away hadn't been against Federer. (Another was against 2005's second-best player, Rafael Nadal.) In Rotterdam's Ahoy Arena, Ljubicic took Federer to a final-set tiebreak that he led 4–2. But the tennis world knows Federer is never beaten until the final point has been won, and he showed it by bouncing back to take his second title of the year.

Federer's third title of the year came in Dubai, again Ljubicic the beaten finalist, again in a third set but this time 6–3. He'd beaten Agassi in the semi-finals – in fact, he played Agassi twice that week, the first time in arguably the most spectacular setting ever for a tennis 'match'.

Dubai is home to the world's only seven-star hotel, the Burj al-Arab. Built on a man-made island in the Gulf of Arabia just off the main settlement of Dubai, the hotel was designed to resemble a graceful sailing boat from a distance. Near the top, at 211m (692ft) above sea level, it boasts its own helipad, a plate-like addition to the structure measuring 415sq/m (1361sq/ft) – almost big enough for a tennis court.

Almost? Why let a few missing metres stop the fun? On this plate, someone had the idea of laying a temporary tennis court and inviting Roger Federer and Andre Agassi to play on it.

And so, on 22 February 2005, Federer and Agassi played a gentle set on the makeshift court. It was a little shorter than a regular tennis court, but the length of the court wasn't of primary concern. It was billed by many in the media as the highest tennis court in the world, which isn't entirely true; Alpine resorts that host tournaments such as Gstaad and Kitzbühel are considerably higher above sea level than 211m, but, with no ground immediately beneath the helipad, it would have felt high enough.

'When I was asked to do this [play tennis on the helipad], I didn't know what to expect,' Federer said. 'The view is absolutely amazing. I've been in Dubai many times and have stayed at the Burj al-Arab before, but this was an absolute treat. To play tennis with Andre on top of such an amazing hotel and overlooking the whole of Dubai was absolutely spectacular.'

The two players were so taken by the experience that they wanted to continue playing, but the hotel had to chase them off because a guest was about to arrive via helicopter and the 'court' had to be cleared.

Before 2005 began, Federer had let it be known that, for the first time since making his debut in 1999, he wouldn't be available for a Davis Cup tie.

There were some raised eyebrows in the offices of the International Tennis Federation, the custodians of tennis's oldest and most prestigious team competition and the sport's overall governing body, which receives a sizeable percentage of its income from Davis Cup profits. To compound concerns, Carlos Moya and Tim Henman – two equally loyal servants of their nations' causes – also announced they would be missing the team variant that year, Henman for good. As it happened, both he and Moya went on to suffer an alarming slump in form, adding to the anecdotal evidence that players who skip the Davis Cup often do their tour form as much harm as good; the different sense of responsibility inherent in playing for one's country appears to give some players a dimension they don't get elsewhere.

The ITF's president, Francesco Ricci Bitti, was a voice of calm. He pointed out that Federer had always turned out, even when Davis Cup ties fell uncomfortably for his tour programme, and it was proper for the tennis community to grant him his break. After some rejigging of the tennis calendar, itself prompted by some rejigging in 2004 to accommodate the Olympic tennis event, the first-round week of the Davis Cup had slipped from the beginning of February to the beginning of March. In 2005, it fell the week before the Masters Series event in Indian Wells, a tournament Federer was prioritising in his bid to remain at the top of the rankings. Besides, he'd withdrawn from only one tie, giving the impression that he'd return for Switzerland's next Davis Cup match – either a quarter-final, if the Federer-less Swiss beat the Netherlands, or a play-off tie in the qualifying round for the 2006 world group if they lost.

More eyebrows were raised when Federer did not turn up in Indian Wells to acclimatise to conditions in the California Desert, as anticipated, but in South Africa, where he was visiting the Roger Federer Foundation-funded Imbewu project. Yet, when the photos of his visit to the project hit the world's newspapers, it was understandable that no one wanted to point out that he was supposed to have withdrawn from the Davis Cup in order to concentrate on the Indian Wells tournament.

Meanwhile, in the picturesque town of Fribourg, the rest of Switzerland's players were determined to prove they could win without their illustrious compatriot. And in the Netherlands, they had a beatable opponent. If Federer had played, the Swiss would almost certainly have won comfortably, but his absence proved a great leveller against another team struggling for survival.

That year, the Dutch were without Martin Verkerk, who had undergone shoulder surgery; their top player, Sjeng Schalken, was on the comeback trail after contracting the strength-sapping condition mononucleosis; so their inspirational captain, Tjerk Bogtstra, had to motivate his other players to punch well above their weight. The result was a tie that proved so exciting that Switzerland's captain, Marc Rosset, said, 'In my fourteen years in the Davis Cup, I have experienced a lot, but this was one of the best weeks. Our comradeship was great, and we have shown that alongside Roger we have other players. We've waited a long time for that.' It was a lovely comment, although it proved to be one of his last as captain.

In a nice twist, Federer's place in the Swiss team was taken by Marco Chiudinelli. After expecting to play tennis just for fun and go to university, Federer's boyhood mate suddenly found himself with a spurt in form in his mid-teens, which prompted him to put his study plans on hold and try to make it as a tennis professional. After two or three meagre years, he finally put in the hard work and surged up the rankings in 2004, earning his Davis Cup call-up in March 2005. 'Roger phoned me a few days before the tie,' says Chiudinelli, 'but we didn't speak much, only for about three minutes. I think he didn't want to say too much. We had coaches in the team, and Marc Rosset was the captain, so I think it was right that he didn't try to add much input. But he sent me a message from South Africa on the day of the tie.'

Chiudinelli had never played a best-of-five-sets match before and fought gamely in his opening rubber against Schalken before succumbing 7–6, 4–6, 6–3, 5–7, 6–2. He was 3–5 down in the fourth set but dug deep to win four games and force a fifth. 'In a normal tour event I wouldn't have won the fourth,' he said afterwards, 'it's like a dream to be on the court with such a fantastic crowd.' A lack of experience meant Chiudinelli dropped the first four games of the final set, and there was no way back after that.

With Chiudinelli injuring his shoulder shortly after the tie and having to undergo surgery, he is hardly someone to whom the Swiss will be looking in the future. But the experience gained by his teammate Stanislas Wawrinka that day was to prove vital. On his debut in a live rubber, he played the Dutch debutant Peter Wessels. The Dutchman ran out a 7–6, 6–7, 7–6, 6–4 winner, but Wawrinka had six set points in the first-set tiebreak and one in the third. If the two had met a few months later, Wawrinka would probably have won the match, such was his rapid rise up the rankings in the remainder of 2005.

Federer's absence ought to have been felt just as sharply

in the doubles, where George Bastl had to stand in for him alongside Yves Allegro, and, when the Swiss lost the first two sets to Wessels and Dennis van Scheppingen, it looked like the tie would be decided by that evening. But Allegro led a spirited fightback in which Switzerland saved two match points in the fourth set and one in the fifth, and they ran out 9–7 winners in a match lasting four and a half hours.

With Wessels struggling with a back problem and doubtful for the fifth singles, it looked like the tie would be decided in the fourth rubber, where Wawrinka was up against Schalken. The Swiss led 4–1 in the fifth set and served for the match at 5–3, but then at 30–15 he got a bad call. 'Only in Switzerland would this happen,' he said later. 'The line judges were so keen to be neutral, they made close decisions against us.' He still managed four match points, and on the second he thought he'd won when a line judge called a Schalken shot out, but the umpire overruled, correctly as it turned out. Once Schalken had saved the fourth with a stunning backhand pass played from behind his baseline, Wawrinka's bolt was shot and the Dutchman won 9–7. Wessels did indeed retire with back problems after a set of the dead rubber, which told the Swiss just how close they had come to winning without their trump card.

The Swiss suffered another close Davis Cup defeat, but this time they came away with real hope for the future. The country was desperate for a quality second singles player, and in Wawrinka it seemed to have found one (even Chiudinelli seemed a possibility at the time but was soon to fall away). And yet... There may have been 'comradeship', as Rosset put it, but the tie had done nothing to enhance the captain's standing with the members of his team. It seemed that Marc Rosset was also under fire.

Before doing anything drastic, however, they sought a chat with Federer. He had a sense of what was going on, having been in regular SMS contact with the Swiss team from South Africa during the weekend. The players knew Federer and Rosset went back a long way, so they sounded him out about his feelings with regard to a change of captain. 'We were all in favour,' recalls Chiudinelli. 'If Roger had been completely against it, Marc would still be captain.' With Federer happy to go along with a change of personnel – albeit keen not to be the instigator – Rosset was removed from the captaincy.

Using the model of the team supremo with a part-time captain, Swiss Tennis appointed Ivo Werner as 'Teamchef' (team boss), with Severin Lüthi as captain. Werner is a Czech-born German coach who coached Jakob Hlasek in the 1990s and took Petr Korda to the Australian Open title and number two in the world rankings in 1998. Lüthi was a promising junior who never quite broke into the top 600, and then became a part-time coach and part-time businessman with a firm selling advertising merchandise at tennis events. He'd been brought into the Swiss set-up by Peter Lundgren for the Morocco tie in September 2002, and had proved himself a popular general aide to the players, who knew him from their junior days. The result was a harmony in the Swiss camp for the following tie against Great Britain that had been absent since the Casablanca tie following Peter Carter's death three years earlier.

Despite the fact that Federer was no longer committing himself to the Davis Cup to quite the same degree that he had in earlier years, there seemed finally to be a sense of discipline and contentment in the Swiss Davis Cup set-up. The team could make great use of Federer, but they weren't totally dependent on him in order to remain a world-group nation. Only if they harboured dreams of winning the competition was his presence still essential.

Federer's decision to concentrate on Indian Wells rather than the Davis Cup paid dividends. Again he came up against Ljubicic, this time in the third round, and beat him on two tiebreaks. When he beat Hewitt to take the title without dropping a set in the entire ten days, he had won four of the five tournaments he'd played since the start of the year.

Then it was on to Miami for the next Masters Series event, where he was up against Tim Henman in the quarter-finals and Agassi in the semis, although neither man had much of a hold on him any more and Federer won both comfortably in straight sets.

In the final, Federer faced Rafael Nadal, the Spaniard who'd been the find of the 2004 Davis Cup year, beating Andy Roddick in the final to help Spain earn their second title. But, as Roddick correctly observed at the time, while the youngster had played some great individual matches, he had yet to string them together. The string was about to begin.

In a superb final, Nadal won the first two sets and then led 4–1 in the third. Federer pegged him back, but when Nadal led 5–3 in the third-set tiebreak, he was just two points from a famous win. But then his lack of experience allowed Federer to win four points on the run, and the Swiss raced away with the fourth and fifth sets for a 2–6, 6–7, 7–6, 6–3, 6–1 win. Nonetheless, the eighteen-year-old left-hander had served notice that he was ready for an assault on the top level of the sport and, by the time he and Federer next met, he was ready to beat him.

When Federer beat Fernando Gonzalez to reach the quarter-finals of the Monte Carlo Masters, he'd gone twenty-five matches unbeaten and had lost just once in his previous fifty-three. The Swiss radio journalist Marco Mordasini makes an observation about Federer: 'I'd go so far as to say that, if he loses a match, it isn't an opponent who has beaten him on tennis grounds but he's lost it for external non-tennis reasons, whatever they may be.' Whether that is true every time, there were certainly external, non-tennis factors at play the day that Federer's latest winning streak came to an end. Whether they accounted for his defeat can, of course, never be proved, but they created a very strange atmosphere for a high-level tennis match.

Nine days earlier, Prince Rainier III, the monarch and ruler of the principality of Monaco, had died. His funeral was scheduled for the day of the Monte Carlo Masters quarter-finals. With dozens of heads of state and government in town, security was tight and a curfew was imposed from breakfast time until mid-afternoon, which meant anyone wanting to go to the Monte Carlo Country Club – the site of the tournament (half of which is actually on French territory) – had to get there early. And, while the view across the Mediterranean from the clubhouse is one of the most spectacular in world tennis, there isn't a lot to do on site, so all the players were somewhat at a loose end. With the overall ambience in Monaco very subdued, it created an eerie atmosphere seldom witnessed at a top-level tennis tournament.

That atmosphere was heightened by a minute's silence before play began. And, although Federer's two-hour-eighteen-minute match against the French teenager Richard Gasquet was a cliffhanger, it was characterised more by nerves and errors than by the glorious aestheticism of both men's elegant strokes.

For Gasquet, that quarter-final provided the potential of a coming-out party. Three years earlier, he'd become the youngest player ever to win a main-draw match at a Masters Series tournament, when he'd come through the Monte Carlo qualifying tournament as a fifteen-year-old and then beaten the fifty-first-ranked Franco Squillari in a first-round three-setter. That success seemed to justify years of being hyped by the press after first appearing as a nine-year-old on the cover of France's principal tennis magazine, which had hailed him as the future of French tennis. Yet, after that breakthrough against Squillari, a series of injuries coupled with a belief that advancing up the rankings would be easier than it is in reality saw him slide out of public view. By now approaching his nineteenth birthday, he was finally working his way back, and in Monte Carlo he had the chance to measure his progress against the best in the world.

Federer broke early but Gasquet soon bounced back, and Federer was ultimately glad to take the first set into the tiebreak. Once there, he stormed to a 7–1 success, which looked to most observers to have broken Gasquet's resistance. But Gasquet broke the Federer serve early in the second set, which he went on to take 6–2, and, when he opened up a 2–0 lead in the final set and held the advantage up to 5–3, a shock result was on the cards. Gasquet then had a match point that he should have won but, having opened up the court for an easy volley, he fluffed it. When Federer then broke back for 4–5, Gasquet's chance looked to have gone. He had a second match point in that tenth game, but Federer saved it.

The tiebreak they played in that third set was full of drama and tension, with neither man able to finish the job. Federer had three match points; the first Gasquet saved with a service winner, but the second and third were squandered on Federer errors.

Gasquet then had his third match point at 9–8, Federer came to the net, and Gasquet ripped a backhand down the line to win the match 7–6, 6–2, 7–6. The shock result announced to the world that Gasquet was likely to become a factor at the top of men's tennis. It also prevented Federer from becoming the first man to win three successive Masters Series tournaments.

But it had been a subdued Federer, and with his energy levels back to normal four weeks later, he showed the true balance of power between him and Gasquet by beating the Frenchman 6–3, 7–5, 7–6 in the Hamburg final, a tournament he won without dropping a set.

Before heading to the French Open, Federer had another appointment. He had been nominated for the top 'Laureus' award, that of world sportsman of the year for 2004. At the awards ceremony he beat off the competition of Lance Armstrong (cycling), Hicham el Guerrouj (athletics), Michael Phelps (swimming), Valentino Rossi (motor cycling) and Michael Schumacher (motor racing) to earn arguably the highest honour in overall world sport. (An interesting footnote is that the world sportsman of the year couldn't quite manage to win the Basel sportsman of the year award! A committee of sports journalists from his home city decided that naming Federer, the winner in 2003, would be boring, so they gave the award to Marcel Fischer, who had won a gold medal in fencing at the Athens Olympics.)

Then it was off to the French Open in Paris, where again he started out as one of the front-line favourites. But, by then, Rafael Nadal was on a phenomenal run of twenty-nine wins in his last thirty clay-court matches, the previous seventeen having brought him the titles in Monte Carlo, Barcelona and Rome. Despite being a threat to Federer's dominance of tennis, Nadal was actually very good news for the world number one. Much as people admire a master craftsman, what gets the pulses racing in sport is a rivalry; people never sickened of the Borg–McEnroe and Evert–Navratilova rivalries of the 1970s and '80s, and the ATP and the media tried their best to build up clashes between Pete Sampras and Andre Agassi into a rivalry in the 1990s (which it was for short periods). The exuberant and ebullient topspin-heavy Nadal – with his pirate-like appearance in sleeveless shirt, plus-four-length shorts and shoulder-length hair – was a wonderful counterfoil to the calm, flat-hitting, neat Federer, and presented the makings of the kind of rivalry from which both could profit immensely.

Tennis fans were licking their lips at the prospect of a Federer–Nadal final, but the Spaniard still wasn't ranked high enough to be seeded second, the position that would have guaranteed he would be kept apart from Federer before the final. Instead, he was seeded fourth, and the draw wasn't in a mood to co-operate – he came out of the hat in the same half as Federer, which meant the two were projected to meet in the semi-finals. That seemed to play into Nadal's hands; Federer had after all won his previous nineteen finals, so most of his main challengers felt the best chance of beating him came in the semis or earlier.

Meanwhile, the draw was also unkind to Federer, who looked like he'd have to face Carlos Moya, David Nalbandian and Nadal before reaching the final. Moya he beat in straight sets in the fourth round, on the same day as the neat but unremarkable Romanian Victor Hanescu beat Nalbandian. Freed from having to face his Argentinian nemesis, Federer beat Hanescu comfortably to reach the semis without having dropped a set since losing to Richard Gasquet in Monte Carlo. As expected, Nadal awaited him.

On the night of his victory over Hanescu, Federer went to the ITF's champions' dinner, an annual black-tie bash staged on the second Tuesday of the French Open to honour the singles, doubles, junior and wheelchair world champions of the previous year. It was his second champions' dinner – he and Jelena Dokic had been the best juniors of 1998 and had received their award at Paris's Hôtel de Ville in June 1999.

It was a slightly off-colour Federer who showed up after beating Hanescu. Nothing of substance can be held against him – he turned up on time, carried out all his obligations, and, when all the speeches and ceremonies were over, he asked the ITF president Francesco Ricci Bitti if he was now free to go. That showed a sense of co-operation and responsibility not shared by some of his predecessors as world champion. And yet something didn't seem to be quite right. He showed up on his own, without his partner, Mirka Vavrinec, despite her having told an ITF official three hours earlier that she'd be there; he turned up unshaven; and, while his dinner jacket was immaculate and his black shoes brightly polished, he had omitted to wear a bow tie, and the top three buttons of his shirt were undone. It might have been just a fashion statement, but it contrasts with his three appearances at the Wimbledon champions' dinner at London's Savoy hotel, when he always shaved beforehand and always wore his bow tie.

Two days later, he walked out on to the Philippe Chatrier Arena at Roland Garros looking somewhat ashen faced to play his semi-final against Nadal. He was entitled to be a little frustrated, given that the most eagerly awaited match of the tournament had been delayed until 6.29pm due to rain and the fact that the first semi-final had gone to five sets. If the Federer–Nadal match had gone to five sets, it would not have been completed that day. There was also an omen in Nadal's favour; the Spaniard was celebrating his nineteenth birthday that day, and four months earlier Federer had been defeated in the semi-finals of the Australian Open by another birthday boy, Marat Safin.

Both men were nervous in the first set, and neither found serving an advantage. In fact, six of the nine games in the first sent went against the serve, with Federer losing a remarkable four out of five, as both men tried to sound each other out. Federer found his form in the second set and at 1–1 looked the stronger player. But Nadal's heavy topspin and use of angles – especially his looped left-handed forehand, which drove Federer well wide of his comfort zone on the backhand wing – was undermining Federer's confidence in his game, which in turn led to him serving poorly and committing an uncharacteristically large number of errors with his normally deadly forehand.

Serving at 2–3 in the third set, Federer was broken from

40–15 up, which proved enough for Nadal to take a two-sets-to-one lead. Federer came out with an early break in the fourth and led 3–1, but still he didn't seem comfortable. At 3–2 he was broken back, and when Nadal held serve to lead 4–3, with the clock striking nine, Federer had a word with the umpire about the light. Had he won the fourth set, they would have had to come back the next day, and maybe Federer would have been more on his game. But Nadal held firm, broke again and won the match 6–3, 4–6, 6–4, 6–3 on Federer's thirty-fifth forehand error of the match.

Later that night, Federer said, 'I had too many highs and lows. He was much more consistent. I started bad and finished bad. I was good in the middle, but it wasn't good enough.'

Federer is adamant he wasn't beaten by anything going on off court. Asked about it six months later, he said, 'There was no problem, and also during the match there were no problems whatsoever. I was even being pushed by the fans, which was exciting. I would have wished that things went better, but there was nothing upsetting me incredibly much, except that I thought they should have stopped the match because of darkness, but they didn't. But again, what can I say as a player? I could have addressed that later to the supervisor, but I didn't do that because the match is over and that's it. I don't want to make a scene here. No, there were no problems leading up to that match.'

Fair enough. At his next tournament, the Gerry Weber

Open in Halle in the first week of June, he again seemed out of sorts. He came very close to losing to the Swedish player Robin Söderling in the first round, and was doing only the minimum of media requirements, including refusing to speak Swiss German in press conferences. Yet round by round his level improved, and he reached the final. There he faced Marat Safin for the first time since their epic encounter in Melbourne four months earlier.

The prospect of facing Safin on grass wouldn't have caused Federer too many sleepless nights. After all, the Russian had left Wimbledon in 2004 after a first-round defeat, saying he never wanted to play on grass again. But the quiet persuasive skills of Peter Lundgren that had done so much to rein in the excesses of Federer's temper had worked their magic on Safin, and a little luck in Halle – notably a saved match point against the Frenchman Fabrice Santoro in the first round – had allowed him to revise his view of grass. By the time he stepped out to play Federer, he was hardly a fan of the sport's original surface, but he had begun to believe in his ability on it. It was to prove a little gem of a final.

After winning the first set, Federer lost his cool at 3–3 in the second, engaging in a long discussion with the umpire after the trembler device that calls lets failed to register on a serve. In the same game, he faced two break points but saved them, only to lose the set on an 8–6 tiebreak as Safin's returning hit its peak. Both players were striking the ball so well by that time that ultimately the only difference between the two was that Federer chose to come to the net on a couple of crucial points, and that helped him gain the crucial break of the final set. 'I really thought I did a good job today by keeping my cool,' he said after his 6–4, 6–7, 6–4 win. 'Even though I lost the second set on the breaker, I felt I was very close to winning it, so I'm very pleased. A good performance all week long, and that's what you want to feel, heading into Wimbledon.'

Most tennis fans would have settled for a repeat Federer–Safin match for the Wimbledon final, but Safin was found out in the third round by the grass-court skills of left-handed Spaniard Feliciano Lopez. Federer went on to claim his third Wimbledon title after dropping just one set, to Nicolas Kiefer in the third round. The final against Andy Roddick promised much but ended with Federer enjoying a straight-sets win 6–2, 7–6, 6–4. 'I'm a better player than I was two years ago and last year,' said the refreshingly frank Roddick after the match, 'but I have nothing to show for it. It's frustrating, but he's better too – head and shoulders better than the rest of us.'

The veteran American journalist Bud Collins, writing a Wimbledon Diary, used typically colourful phrasing to describe Federer's dominance: 'Federer was playing a game called run-sheep-run with Roddick as the scrambling lamb eventually getting shorn, just as Lleyton Hewitt had been in the semi-finals. Roger, constantly varying his farm tools, has so many ways to hit a tennis ball in so many directions, with so many shifting spins and speeds, that the best Roddick could hope for was to catch up with some of them. But far from enough.'

And still Federer continued to charm the tennis world in three languages. At the end of a long press conference at Wimbledon, when someone shouted to him across the departing journalists, 'Roger, are there any more languages you speak?' he replied, 'If I did I wouldn't tell you, or my press conferences would take even longer.'

With his Wimbledon victory in 2005, Federer had gone thirty-six matches unbeaten on grass, putting him within striking distance of Björn Borg's run of forty-one, posted between 1976 and 1981. Perhaps more significantly, he had reached the same stage Pete Sampras got to around 1998 – he had become so good that some of his major titles were becoming less memorable. In winning the Wimbledon final that year, he said he felt his display against Roddick was better than the way he'd played against Lleyton Hewitt in the 2004 US Open final, which was viewed by many as his greatest single match. He was beginning to transcend the excellence barrier into that realm where many people don't really appreciate the heights a player is scaling simply because he or she scales them so often. It was a problem he was to run into with his compatriots later in the year.

Federer's decision not to play in Gstaad allowed him to go home for the first time following a Wimbledon triumph. It also allowed him to appear at a civic reception in Basel, and greet 3,000 of his fans by brandishing his miniature replica of Wimbledon's gold trophy from the balcony of the 'Roothuus' city hall. The 'Roothuus' is perhaps the most striking building in Basel; built of sandstone in the early sixteenth century, it has a deep-red colour, which acts as a beautiful contrast to the brightly coloured and partly gilded pagan figures which form an adornment to the late Gothic architecture. A total of 3,000 fans may not sound much, but in a land where worshipping sporting heroes is not part of the national culture it is sizeable, the more so given that the reception took place during working hours.

The main reason for the reception was to recognise the contribution Federer has made in putting Basel on the map. But what the people of Basel value more about him than his presence or his Wimbledon titles is his normality. They will forgive him if he can't play the Swiss Indoors once or twice; it's his willingness to chat with people that scores most in such civic receptions.

Federer took another off-court decision after Wimbledon 2005. Two years after splitting with the player-management company IMG, he decided to seek their part-time help. To some it was an admission of failure for the independent company Roger Federer Management, but that would be too simplistic an assessment. Federer and his entourage had decided that their priority would be his international standing – not Swiss, not European. For that, they reasoned, they needed international help, so they went back to the firm they'd jettisoned two years earlier and entered a deal in which IMG would be responsible for marketing him internationally. On a personal level, he was assigned the IMG agent Tony Godsick – the husband of the former French Open finalist Mary-Joe Fernandez – whose other clients included another popular and eloquent world number one: Lindsay Davenport.

After Wimbledon, Federer opted not to play another tournament until the Masters Series event in Cincinnati, missing the Montreal Masters, which Nadal won. With the Canadian tournament, six of the nine Masters Series tournaments had been played, and Federer and Nadal had shared all six between them, becoming in the process numbers one and two in the world and threatening men's tennis with a seemingly unshakeable duopoly. So, when Federer beat Roddick in the Cincinnati final, the American was no longer the principal challenger. The result left Federer's head-to-head with Roddick at 10–1, and Roddick seemed to be getting left behind.

And nothing that happened at the US Open in New York changed that impression. Roddick was stunned in the opening round by Gilles Müller, the only player of note to have come from Luxembourg, who beat the US number one on three tiebreaks to silence not only the American public but also the reams of advertising material on which Roddick had appeared in the run-up to the tournament. Federer, meanwhile, was good value for the admission money, playing a highly entertaining match against Fabrice Santoro in the second round, before going on to face Olivier Rochus, who'd been his doubles partner in his junior Wimbledon triumph, in the third. Both men came close to taking a set, but Federer scraped home in three in both matches. But he did drop a set in the fourth round, to the same player who had taken a set off him at

Wimbledon, Nicolas Kiefer. People were starting to take notice of Kiefer, for it was becoming the case that, if you could win a set against Federer, you were worth a fair bit of attention and admiration.

Whenever Federer plays David Nalbandian, the head-to-head is always quoted. In advance of their quarter-final in New York, Nalbandian led 5–2 and, while Federer had won the previous two, they hadn't played for twenty months, since the 2004 Australian Open. On this occasion it was to be no contest. Federer lifted his level to win for the loss of just seven games, while Nalbandian played a poor match.

By this time, the New York public was getting excited about Andre Agassi's run to the quarter-finals. He'd missed Wimbledon after a back problem had flared up at the French Open that required him to have a cortisone injection. He had done well at two of the North American hard-court tournaments, but few dared hope that he could go all the way at the US Open. Nevertheless, he was through to the quarter-finals and, after coming back from the brink of defeat to beat the revitalised James Blake on a final-set tiebreak in one of the matches of the year, he and Federer were each just one match away from a dream final.

Federer had to deal with Lleyton Hewitt in one semi-final and, despite dropping the third set, he did so without ever being truly threatened. In the other, Agassi had to go to five sets for the third match running, this time against Robby Ginepri, but none of his matches had been particularly long, so he would hardly enter the final hampered by exhaustion.

Though there was less than twenty-four hours between the end of the semi-finals and the first point of the final, the match was the talk of New York. When they finally began playing at 4.30pm on a sunny September Sunday, Federer struck first. He won the first set, but Agassi broke in the second game of the second set to signal his intention to make a fight of it. A second break allowed the American to level at a set all, and the crowd was right into the match. When Agassi broke to lead 4–2 in the third set, the crowd was going wild at the prospect of a sentimental victory for their thirty-five-year-old hero. An upset was a genuine possibility.

But that was Federer's cue to find some of his best form of the tournament. He broke straight back, almost broke in the eleventh game and then stormed through the tiebreak 7–1.

From then on, Agassi was a beaten man and, when, at 5–0 in the fourth set, Federer played a slack game, one could be forgiven for suspecting that a sense of charity had crept quietly into Federer's mind, so Agassi's last set of the tournament – possibly his last set ever at the US Open – wouldn't end 6–0. It made the final score 6–3, 2–6, 7–6, 6–1 to Federer.

Agassi's parting words to the Flushing Meadows crowd were: 'Thank you, New York. It's been a great twenty years.' But it's what he said in his post-match press conference that carries most weight.

By winning his sixth Grand Slam title, Federer had equalled the number of majors won by Boris Becker and Stefan Edberg. 'That's fantastic,' he said, 'tying your idols. Isn't that great? It's every boy's dream, and I made it come true today in a memorable final.'

But Agassi was not talking about equality. 'There's only so long you can go on denying it: he's the best player I've ever played against,' he said. 'Pete [Sampras] was great, no question, but there was a place to get to with Pete. You knew what you had to do. If you did it, it could be on your terms. There's no such place like that with Roger. There's a sense of urgency on every point, on every shot. If you do what you're supposed to do, you feel like it gives you a *chance* to win the point. That's just too good. He plays the game in a very special way that I haven't seen before.'

Federer felt the American's praise was a little over the top. 'The best player of this generation, yes,' he accepted when Agassi's comments were put to him, 'but nowhere close to the best ever. Just look at the records that some guys have. I'm a little cookie.'

Modesty as a polite shield for immense self-belief is central to the Federer make-up. He knew, of course, that he was more than a little cookie; he was resorting to statistics, when what Agassi was saying was that statistics cannot do justice to what Federer brings to a tennis court. When people in later years argue in tennis bars over who's the greatest tennis player of all time, Agassi's words will carry immense weight in separating Federer from Sampras.

Despite the general impression early in 2005 that he'd be missing just one Davis Cup tie that year, Federer took his time to confirm that he would turn out for Switzerland in its promotion/relegation play-off battle against Great Britain in Geneva. He eventually agreed to play, even though it meant a week on clay between the end of the North American hard-court season and the start of the Asian and European indoor swing.

Against the British, his status as the runaway world number one actually worked against him. Lacking their top-ranked player, Tim Henman, the visitors figured – logically – that, if they were to beat the Swiss, they had to win the two singles matches Federer wasn't playing and try to sneak the doubles. So, in order to engineer the situation where Greg Rusedski and Andy Murray would play Switzerland's number two, Stanislas Wawrinka, on the days they wanted, the visitors threw in Alan Mackin as a sacrificial lamb to face Federer on the opening day. Mackin, ranked 262nd, will be able to tell his grandchildren that he won two games against the best of his generation (if not the best ever), but it was a match Federer had won on his reputation alone before even stepping on to the court. It was a non-contest.

The other match Federer played that weekend was the doubles with Yves Allegro, against Greg Rusedski and Andy Murray, which was much more competitive. But with Wawrinka having beaten Murray the previous day, the British plan had failed and the sting had gone out of the tie. Federer and Allegro won in four sets to secure Switzerland's place in the 2006 world group.

Four days later, the draw for 2006 was made. It gave the Swiss an attractive home tie against Australia, which was not only winnable but would also be for the Peter Carter Trophy. Yet Federer was to keep everyone waiting until the last minute before deciding whether to play, and then he said no, citing the need to recuperate following his exertions in winning the 2006 Australian Open.

For the British, the Davis Cup tie against Switzerland came a week too early. The following week, Andy Murray – still eighteen – reached the final in Bangkok, enjoying the best week of his first year as a professional. Awaiting him there was Federer, who had opted to follow his 2004 post-US Open routine of playing a tournament and then having a holiday. The Swiss won the final 6–3, 7–5, a scoreline that gave Murray hope for the future, although Federer's eleventh title of the year was never seriously in doubt.

With such dominance of his sport, surely 2005 would be his year finally to win the Swiss Indoors in Basel!

A few days after returning from Asia, Federer was practising at the *Paradies* club owned by the Swiss Indoors' impresario Roger Brennwald. He was hitting with the rising Swiss player Michael Lammer, a contemporary of Federer's who had just had his breakthrough by qualifying for the US Open and reaching the second round. As the *Basler Zeitung* journalist Freddy Widmer reported in his short book *Moments '05*, on that occasion Federer had tried to book a court, only to find they'd all been taken. But then a genial octogenarian Ernst Schneider – the lifelong driving force behind the cigar and luxury-goods company Davidoff, which has sponsored the Swiss Indoors for many years – offered to give up the court he'd booked to allow Federer to practise. According to Widmer, somehow a bit of water had got on to the surface and, while playing a cross-court forehand, Federer slipped and crashed to the ground. A subsequent X-ray revealed he'd torn a tendon in his right foot.

Three weeks later, Brennwald was faced with the same unpopular task he'd had a year earlier: he had to tell his loyal public that the man they really wanted to see at Basel wouldn't be competing for the second year running.

Following the X-ray, Federer's entourage began a race to get him ready for the Tennis Masters Cup, which in 2005 returned to Shanghai. Federer has always had a soft spot for Asia, and agreed to go to Shanghai after his triumph in Bangkok to take part in the official opening of the Qi Zhong Stadium, a purpose-built 15,000-seater state-of-the-art arena with a beautiful retractable roof made of eight interlocking petals. Now there was a serious danger that he wouldn't be able to compete in the event the stadium was built for.

Less than three weeks before the Tennis Masters Cup was due to begin, Federer was still on crutches, but some careful yet intensive rehabilitation work with Pierre Paganini got him healthy just in time to take part. It was the same as in 2004: he was fit, but was he match-fit? His opening match against David Nalbandian would give some indication.

Federer took to the court with a brace round his right

ankle – a precaution, he said, more a comfort blanket than a real need – and when he took the first set against the Argentinian everything looked fine. But Nalbandian bounced back to win the second and, when he led 3–1 in the third, it was looking grim for the tournament. The round-robin format means Federer could have lost and still qualified for the semi-finals but, with Marat Safin, Andy Roddick and Lleyton Hewitt all absent, the organisers were desperate for him to survive. He did, winning the final set 6–4, a result that was to prove an immense relief for the city, as Andre Agassi and Rafael Nadal pulled out a day later with injuries, leaving the Shanghai officials feeling they had severely lost face. (Losing face is a serious embarrassment in China; in the absence of five illustrious names, Federer was effectively carrying the responsibility for the public credibility of the tournament.)

Following his triumph against Nalbandian, Federer was again up against Ivan Ljubicic in their fifth match of the year. It proved their third to go to three sets and their second to be decided on a final-set tiebreak – but again Federer won, and with it he secured his place in the semi-finals.

In the semis, he came up against Gaston Gaudio, who had said the day before that he didn't really know how he could beat Federer. He proved that by failing to win a game! Federer notched up the first 6–0, 6–0 win of his career, the Argentinian having lost heart early in the second set of what was only a 50-minute match.

By reaching the final, Federer had done what the organisers in Shanghai had hoped: he had appeared in a maximum five matches, and had helped deflect attention from the five high-profile withdrawals. And he then ensured that the 2005 Tennis Masters Cup would for ever be remembered for its best-of-five-sets final rather than for those who didn't show up.

When Federer led his opponent, David Nalbandian, by two sets to love, the match seemed to have been won, but it had taken him two hours and twenty minutes, the second-set tiebreak had been 13–11, and both players had done a lot of running. Instead of building on the momentum of winning the second-set tiebreak to plough home to victory, Federer suddenly began to feel very tired. The ankle wasn't a problem – or so he said – but the six weeks of practice and match time he'd missed while convalescing were beginning to take their toll. The turnaround was dramatic – Nalbandian took sixteen of the next nineteen games to open up a 4–0 lead in the final set. Federer looked beaten.

While few would associate him with the kind of fighting qualities for which Jimmy Connors and Lleyton Hewitt are known, Federer is a fighter. Because he manages his energy so efficiently and can play strokes that look effortless, it seldom looks as if he's digging deep. But he does, and he did that day. He fought his way back to 4–4, and when he broke to lead 6–5 he was serving for a third successive Masters Cup title. At 30–0 it seemed all over. Asked what he was thinking at that point, Nalbandian said, 'I can't go home like this!' And he wouldn't. He played four great points to break back and force a final-set tiebreak, and after a couple of points he was never behind, and won the tiebreak 7–3 to post the biggest win of his career.

That defeat meant that Federer was denied the opportunity to share a remarkable statistic with John McEnroe. In 1984, McEnroe so dominated world tennis that he lost just three matches out of the eighty-five he played that year. The final in Shanghai was Federer's eighty-fifth match of the year, and he went into it having won eighty-one and lost three; a victory would have meant tying McEnroe's phenomenal record. As it was, he finished on eighty-one wins and four losses, but with possible extraneous circumstances surrounding all four of his defeats in 2005. Nevertheless, it was a truly phenomenal year for Federer, in which he posted a consistency that outshines the fact that he 'only' won two Grand Slam titles, compared with the three he won the previous year.

Yet such subtleties aren't always appreciated by the person in the street. And the Swiss can be a tough people to please.

After his heroics of 2004, those of 2005 probably seemed no better, or even slightly worse. When it came to the poll for the Swiss sportsperson of the year, Federer was beaten by Tom Lüthi, Switzerland's world motorcycling champion. Half of the poll is voted for by Switzerland's sports journalists in advance, while the other half is determined by the public via telephone voting during a televised awards gala.

Federer had won the award in 2003 and 2004, so in 2005 was going for his third in a row. In a three-way battle between himself, Lüthi and the ice-skating world champion Stéphane Lambiel, Federer led with forty-two per cent of the ballots after the journalists had made their choice. But the spectacle of Lüthi – who in 2004 was known more for his crashes, but who kept his bike upright in 2005 to claim the 125cc world championship at the age of nineteen – swayed many members of the public, and he edged out Federer. It was clearly no snub to Federer, who took it well.

If there was a minor consolation, it came not in his third successive nomination for the Laureus Award – although that in itself must have been immensely satisfying, and he went on to win the principal Laureus honour for the second year running – but in being named as one of 'the twenty sexiest men alive' by *People* magazine. When that particular accolade was announced during the Tennis Masters Cup, Federer was more amused by it than anything else, but for a man who had won the highest honours the sporting world can bestow, having the attractiveness of his masculinity recognised was probably a more meaningful award than being Swiss sportsperson of the year would have been.

In 2006, Federer's second Australian Open – his seventh Grand Slam – will probably be remembered more for his emotional response to lifting the trophy than for much of his tennis. After receiving the Norman Brookes Trophy from Rod Laver, the only man to win all four majors in a calendar year with everyone eligible to play, Federer walked up to the microphone, said to the crowd, 'I think you know how much this means to me,' and promptly burst into tears. Although he did manage to reach the end of his speech, in which he thanked the necessary dignitaries and sponsors, he did so with a quivering voice that clearly endeared him to the Melbourne faithful, just as it had won over the Wimbledon crowd two and a half years earlier.

In some ways, Federer was lucky at the first Grand Slam of 2006, in that the two players most able to damage him, Marat Safin and Rafael Nadal, were both absent through injury. Also, during a fortnight when the temperature reached forty-four degrees Celsius, he had the good fortune to play five of his seven matches – the last five – at night when some of the heat had gone out of the day. But neither factor should be allowed to detract from a victory that said much about his resilience under pressure.

In truth, he didn't play consistently well throughout the tournament – his backhand was unusually erratic, and his volleys were at best unreliable and at worst poor – but he did what all great champions do: he played well when he needed to most. He won his first three matches in straight sets, and when a 6–0 set gave him a two-sets lead against a highly impressive Tommy Haas in the fourth round, he looked invincible. But from that point, he lost his way a little, and Haas was unlucky to lose that match in five sets.

In the quarter-finals, Federer should have gone two-sets-to-one down against Nikolay Davydenko, yet he played his best tennis of that match on the five set points Davydenko had in the third set, and stormed away in the fourth. It was almost as if the early part of sets had lost their interest for him; only when facing situations of acute danger did he find his best form. He admitted later that, after the second set against Haas, he never quite found a sustained level for the rest of the tournament.

He dropped another set in his semi-final against Nicolas Kiefer, and could have gone two sets down in the final against the twenty-one-year-old Cypriot Marcos Baghdatis, for whom that Australian Open was a breakthrough event. Ultimately, Baghdatis didn't quite believe he could do it, Federer played his best tennis at the end of the second set, and then powered ahead to win eleven games on the run and put himself out of reach.

When Federer won 5–7, 7–5, 6–0, 6–2 to secure his second title in the Rod Laver Arena, there was Laver himself to present the trophy. That would have been enough reason to get emotional. Another reason would have been the presence of Diana and Bob Carter in Federer's own enclosure; Federer had invited the parents of his former coach, Peter, as his guests for the final. It also emerged later that he had been suffering more pain than he was admitting to in the right foot he injured in Basel three months earlier – that would have been another reason for a high degree of emotional satisfaction. But, when asked afterwards why the tears had flowed on the podium, Federer gave an answer that was almost banal: 'When I saw that [Baghdatis] was cramping on his calf muscle [early in the fourth set], and knowing I was in very good shape, so many things go through your head about the win already because you think, "Well, now nothing can go wrong." But, as we saw, it was still quite a long way to the finish line. I was getting emotionally ready for that, which I shouldn't, but I can't block it out. I'm also just human. And I guess, when I won, I was so relieved that I got it through. I wasn't emotional in the first minute, just relieved. It only came out later, when I was standing there with Marcos waiting for the ceremony. I was very relaxed. But once I got up on stage, it all changed.'

Who knows what brought on the tears? In Ancient Greece, the original Olympic athletes were extremely competitive, and it wasn't considered a sign of softness or effeminacy for men who had lost a race or a contest to cry or get very angry; in fact, it was considered quite normal. And for a man like Federer who has subverted most of his boyhood emotions in the quest to be the best in the world and who consequently gives little away during matches, no one should be really surprised if the emotions run free when the discipline is allowed to fall. The tears also allow people to respond to him as a human being. It just doesn't quite seem plausible that the intensity of emotion he expressed should all have been because of victory taking slightly longer to complete than he expected. But maybe he was just protecting himself by giving that answer.

Being such a dominant world number one inevitably attracts scrutiny into all aspects of his game. There were those in Melbourne in January 2006 who were looking for chinks in his armour, signs that he might be about to embark on the kind of slump that often results from a lengthy period of dominance, just as the golfer Tiger Woods suffered a lapse in form after his spectacular ascent to the top. There were enough challenges in Melbourne for Federer to keep any such signs at bay, but, interestingly, he said in a series of interviews at the end of 2005 that his goal for 2006 was to 'stay number one' – not to win the French Open, his one remaining unconquered Slam; not to win the Davis Cup, the ultimate team prize; and not to add something extra to his repertoire. He just wanted to stay number one. It was easy to get the sense that his continued motivation depended as much on players like Nadal, Safin and possibly Baghdatis being around to offer challenging opposition, rather than their being absent through injury and thus giving him a clear run.

A golden opportunity for Federer to celebrate his Australian Open victory on home soil presented itself eleven days later with Switzerland's Davis Cup tie against Australia in Geneva. But again, Federer left his countryfolk on tenterhooks. As the official nominations were announced ten days before the opening day of the Davis Cup weekend, Federer's name wasn't among them. He then issued a statement saying he wanted to play in Switzerland, but he also needed to rest his body. For three days, he gave the impression that he might play, only to decide finally that he needed to take a break, announcing his withdrawal not just from the Davis Cup tie but also from the following week's tournament in Rotterdam.

As Federer left Melbourne to return to Switzerland, he and everyone else were well aware of his place in history.

When asked after his victory at the Rod Laver Arena whether he'd one day like a stadium to be named after him, he replied, 'Yeah, it would be nice, but I don't think I'll get one at a Grand Slam. I don't expect anything like a court named after me. I'm not playing the game because of that, but obviously it would be nice.' Perhaps understandably, the gesture by the Old Boys Basel tennis club to rename their main court the 'Platz Roger Federer' didn't quite register with him.

The goal of 'staying number one' in 2006 was virtually completed by the beginning of April. The body rested, Federer returned to action in Dubai, where he suffered his first defeat of the year in the final to Rafael Nadal; it was the Spaniard's third victory in three matches over the world number one, suggesting he had something on Federer in one-to-one combat. And that impression was reinforced when Nadal posted his fourth and fifth wins over Federer, with a four-sets win in the Monte Carlo final and a glorious five-sets win in a five-hour Rome final, in which Federer had two match points. But the still nineteen-year-old Mallorcan was a long way short of matching his rival's consistency on the tour, and Federer took the first two Masters Series titles of the year in Indian Wells and Miami. That put him 2,465 points ahead of Nadal in the rankings (7,010 to 4,545) going into the French Open, the kind of deficit that can only be overhauled through Federer suffering a serious injury requiring a break of several months.

Before returning home from America after his win over

Ivan Ljubicic in the Miami final, Federer had an appointment at the United Nations headquarters in New York. In the presence of the UN Secretary General Kofi Annan, he was named a 'goodwill ambassador' for the UN children's agency Unicef. The official line was that it was a recognition of the interest in children he had shown through the Roger Federer Foundation, but the link to the foundation was probably of peripheral importance. By 2006, Federer had nothing more to prove in tennis, and his caring attitude to those less fortunate than himself, coupled with a belief that he has been dealt a very fortuitous hand in life, made him an ideal target for one of the highest-profile children's welfare organisations in the world. 'I've been lucky in life, and able to pursue my passion for tennis since I was six years old,' he said as he joined the ranks of goodwill ambassadors that have included David Beckham, Shakira, Youssou N'dour, Vanessa Redgrave, Roger Moore and the late Danny Kaye and Audrey Hepburn. 'It's important to me to help the many children throughout the world who do not have the basic resources they need.'

It seemed a small step on the road to a form of statesmanship Federer seems cut out for when he finally finishes playing tennis.

12

SO WHO EXACTLY *is* Roger Federer? The question can be asked and answered on several levels: his place in tennis history, his place in sport, his place beyond the boundaries of sport, his place in Switzerland, his character, and what we can expect of him in the future, both for the rest of his playing career and after his retirement. And it's also worth asking, just what is it that makes him so successful?

In tennis terms, there's no question he's the best in the world. Having won a seventh Grand Slam singles title at twenty-four, he is clearly one of history's great players, and Andre Agassi's comment after the 2005 US Open final implies Federer may already be in a category above Pete Sampras, who would make most people's list of the five greatest players in the history of lawn tennis.

Many tennis fans love to discuss who they believe is the

greatest player of all time. It's a question that's virtually impossible to answer, as from the 1930s until tennis went 'open' in 1968 – the decades when the sport was divided into split amateur and professional circuits – the greatest amateur players won the most prestigious tournaments (ie the Grand Slams), and, once they'd made their name, they turned professional, earning their living playing exhibition matches but making themselves ineligible for the Grand Slams, Davis Cup and other events. In addition, the sport was for years very much the preserve of a certain affluent social elite, and only in the past thirty years has it really become open to a wider social spectrum. It's therefore impossible to say how great the great names really were relative to each other, and one could make the case that any of Bill Tilden, Donald Budge, Jack Kramer, Lew Hoad, Ken Rosewall, Rod Laver, Björn Borg, John McEnroe, Pete Sampras, Andre Agassi and now Roger Federer were all the greatest ever. It's all a little meaningless, anyway, because certainly the first five on that list won many of their greatest triumphs when the best players were ineligible to compete against them, so they would have to be judged on the basis of incomplete competition.

But it's possible Federer might be on the way to achieving so much that he elevates himself above the variables in the equation. He has dominated his era to date in a way that only Sampras did in the mid-1990s and McEnroe did for a year in 1984. He has played with an elegance that attracts people sometimes ambivalent about tennis, and his eloquence in three languages gives him a statesmanlike quality that McEnroe, Sampras and Agassi could never approach (that shouldn't be held against those brought up without a workable second language, but there's no doubt Federer has a radiance that only McEnroe's volatility could eclipse in the public consciousness).

The elegance with which Federer plays his tennis stems from the fact that his strokes are a modern version of the classic technique that evolved in the era of wooden rackets (he has described his own playing style as 'modern retro'), and it might well have protected his body from the punishment endured by some players with modern technique. While it's too early to be sure, the pounding that his hips and lower back take while playing his groundstrokes might well have been reduced by the much lesser degree of exaggerated body rotation that normally comes with the two-handed backhands and heavily topspun, wristy forehands that characterise modern top-level tennis. (On his backhand, he has been quoted as saying, 'Two-handed backhand for me? Utterly unthinkable. I couldn't do it. The ball would fly over the roof of the stadium. I wouldn't even be in the top 100.' Believe it if you will.)

And he also makes it look so easy. In *Moments '05*, the Swiss journalist Freddy Widmer writes, 'Federer's game makes it look as if his side of the court is smaller and the opponent's side is bigger, and that he has more time to play his shots than his opponent. You're almost tempted to tear up the rulebook and give the opponent two bounces of the ball to Federer's one, just to be fair. In many situations

Federer seems to know what his opponent should be doing well before his opponent realises this for himself.'

At the time of writing, Federer still lacks two major tennis titles: the French Open and the Davis Cup. It might well be that the Davis Cup will forever remain out of his reach, for reasons outside his control, given that Switzerland may never produce a second player to share the load. But, then again, if Switzerland were to win it with Federer taking twelve matches in a year, and thus requiring only a viable doubles partner, such a single-handed victory would certainly enhance his claim to greatness.

He can probably never really be described as 'the greatest ever' until he wins the French Open. The four major tournaments in tennis are much more a test of versatility than they were when Rod Laver won the first and so far only 'open' Grand Slam in 1969 (then three of the four were on grass), so one could argue that by winning majors on two different surfaces – grass and hard – Federer has equalled Laver's achievement. But the red clay of Paris demands vastly different qualities of a player than the grass of Wimbledon, the concrete hard court of the US Open and the rubberised hard court of the Australian Open, so, until Federer wins in Paris, he will be vulnerable to unfavourable comparisons with Hoad, Rosewall, Laver, Borg and Agassi, who all won on both clay and grass. On today's ultra-competitive global circuit, it's probably asking too much for a player to win all four Grand Slams in a calendar year, but a 'career Grand Slam' is still achievable and ought to be Federer's next target.

There's one other achievement that would enhance his place in history: an Olympic gold medal. He missed out in 2004, but as long as he remains fit and hungry he ought to have two more bites of the cherry: on the hard courts of Beijing in 2008, and on the grass of Wimbledon in 2012, which he has already suggested might be a highly appropriate event on which to end his career.

How big is Roger Federer outside the world of tennis? This question needs to be considered on two levels: elsewhere in sport and in the non-sporting world in general.

Elsewhere in sport, Federer is recognised as one of the true greats of our time. The fact that he's been nominated in 2003, 2004 and 2005 for the Laureus Sportsman of the Year Award, winning it for his achievements in 2004 and 2005, confirms his standing among his sporting peers. He doesn't have the emotional attraction of someone like Lance Armstrong, who was told he had less than a fifty-fifty chance of surviving advanced testicular cancer that had spread to his brain and lungs but came back to win the Tour de France seven times, or the political dimension of a Muhammad Ali, who became a standard-bearer for African-Americans in the USA. But in terms of his achievements in what is a highly competitive open field, he is fully recognised within the sporting community.

To what extent he is a household name that transcends sport is more open to question. In a country like Great Britain, which feasts on tennis en masse for two weeks a year when Wimbledon comes around, he is well known, having won what for most is *the* tennis tournament three times, but elsewhere he doesn't score highly outside sport. For instance, the day after his emphatic win over Lleyton Hewitt in the 2004 US Open final, the majority of tennis pictures in the American press were still of Roddick and Agassi (many of them appearing in advertising, but that only reinforces the point).

In the early 1980s, the British satirical television programme *Not the Nine O'Clock News* performed a sketch that seemed to sum up John McEnroe, then at the height of his playing career. Entitled 'Breakfast in the McEnroe Household', it portrayed McEnroe coming down to breakfast, hyperactively gulping down some orange juice and being ticked off my his mother for slurping. 'What did I do?' pleaded the McEnroe character incredulously, thereby triggering a domestic row that mirrored his rages with umpires. Even the modern dancer Wayne Sleep had a routine that portrayed McEnroe's anger in balletic form. Such instances reflect a player transcending the boundaries of sport, and there have been few of them so far associated with Federer.

Martina Navratilova transcended sporting boundaries with her forthright social views, in particular those on matters of sexual orientation and the environment. Thus far, the only opinions Federer has expressed publicly have been strictly within the realms of tennis – for example, voicing strong opposition to the US Open's plan to introduce line-calling technology that would give players the right to appeal against dubious decisions. Perhaps rightly for a twenty-four-year-old with arguably a limited view of the real world, he has refrained from offering controversial views on global issues. However, if one day he makes some forthright comment on, say, the unacceptability of severe poverty in the twenty-first century – perhaps prompted by his close association with the Imbewu project in South Africa or his status as a Unicef ambassador – he will elevate himself to a level where he becomes an important figure outside sporting confines.

How does Federer fit in in Switzerland? Well, for a start, he still lives there, which is more than can be said for a large number of tennis players and their home countries. There is a colony of a couple of hundred tennis players registered to live in Monaco, largely for tax reasons, and there are plenty who flee their homeland because they can't walk down the street without being molested by fans and autograph hunters.

'There isn't the adulation and adoration for him here,' says his former primary-school head teacher, Theresa Fischbacher. 'Perhaps that's why he can still afford to live in Switzerland.'

The Basel journalist Thomas Wirz goes further: 'The Swiss don't like top stars. When the first Roger Federer fan club was opened in Allschwil [a suburb of Basel], I thought there would be a storm of fans, but it was very intimate. I think it has less to do with Basel and more to do with Switzerland.'

There are certainly no plaques around Federer's old childhood haunts, and it wasn't until he'd won three Grand Slam titles that the Old Boys club put up a portrait of him in the clubhouse and renamed Court 1 the Roger Federer Court. 'It hangs together with the reticence of the Swiss to respect people who make their living from sport,' says Niki von Vary, a former teammate of Federer's at Old Boys who is now a political adviser. 'You saw it with Marc Rosset. Whatever you may think of him, he won an Olympic gold medal, but there's no monument or plaque to him. The same with [the top-level Swiss skier] Bernhard Russi. However much sportsmen and -women achieve at the highest level, they don't earn the same reputation that they do in America or Australia or other European nations. It'll certainly come, but it'll take at least a decade. And it's hard to imagine a cult like that of David Beckham. The typical Swiss citizen is so grounded, so connected to the land, he doesn't want to stand out from the crowd; he just wants to come through life without creating a scene. That's the history of Switzerland. It's always been that way and, to a large extent, will always be that way. You see it in politics, with Switzerland's attitude to the EU. We don't have a star culture, and as a result we haven't had a boom like Boris Becker created in Germany. The Swiss are probably too low-key for that.'

All the coaches interviewed for this book were asked if they thought the Federer factor had increased interest in tennis in the Basel area. All could point to the enthusiasm that many youngsters there today have for Federer and their wish to play like him, but few have much evidence that youngsters gifted in several sports are being attracted to tennis because of the inspiration of Roger Federer. Even

Christoph Eymann, a councillor who chairs the Basel education committee, says there has been 'no discernible Basel tennis boom'.

'For us Swiss, only the best is good enough,' says the radio journalist Marco Mordasini. 'Whether it's in sport, in the economy, in politics – when someone begins something, they're interesting, but, once people realise there's a consistency of performance, people lose interest. That's why it's now become very hard for me to get radio stations interested in Federer before the quarter-finals of tournaments, but then we had the same problem with Hingis once she got to the top. Roger is inevitably going to polarise people, anyone who's that successful is going to create some envy. But he will remain a symbol for Switzerland even twenty or thirty years after he stops playing.'

At least Federer had a number of top-level Swiss players to prepare the ground for him, without whom his status in Switzerland might have been much less. Jakob Hlasek breaking into the top ten in 1988 generated the first real interest in tennis, Marc Rosset's Olympic gold medal in 1992 and Switzerland's run to the Davis Cup final that same year further entrenched the sport in the Swiss sporting psyche, and then Martina Hingis became world number one in 1997, just as the golden age of Swiss skiing was coming to an end. But the Swiss were nonetheless slow to really embrace tennis.

Marco Mordasini, whose income depends on how much Swiss radio stations believe tennis will interest their listeners, says, 'The Swiss tend to wait until they really can't afford not to watch. It took a while before we got into tennis, the way it took a while for us to get into the Americas Cup – people really only began to watch [the victory of the Swiss yacht *Alinghi*] when it was such a big story that they couldn't afford not to. There was also a reluctance to accept Hingis. Because she was born outside Switzerland and never spoke a completely clean Swiss German, the Swiss arrogance came to the fore, with people never viewing her as a fully home-baked Swiss – until she started winning, of course, and then she became the "Swiss Miss". I thought it was an appalling way to treat her, especially as Hingis never hesitated to play Fed Cup for Switzerland and should always have been seen as one hundred per cent Swiss.'

As a born-and-bred Swiss who ascended to the top after the Swiss public had served its tennis apprenticeship, Federer has enjoyed more favour from his compatriots than Hingis, and than Patty Schnyder, the other Basel player to have made it to the top ten. But, short of doing a pure Grand Slam (winning all four Grand Slam titles in the same calendar year) or steering Switzerland to the Davis Cup, it's hard to see what he can do that will impress the Swiss any more than they have been impressed to date.

What is Roger Federer like as a person? He's not into alcohol or fast cars, preferring instead to play cards or computer games; he's scared of bungee jumping and sky-diving (he says he was only able to play on the helipad of the Burj al-Arab hotel in Dubai 'because it's not moving');

and he's a very fast SMS text messager. In an interview quoted on the website tennis-x.com, he described himself as 'a funny guy. I'm outgoing. You can have a lot of fun with me. I can hang out.' (Incidentally, that same interview quoted him as saying, 'I've got this thing when I'm sleeping – I don't know if I should say this – but I've this problem of banging my head against the pillow if I'm lying on my stomach. I don't know what it is, but I've been doing this since I was a baby. I really would like to know why and where it comes from. It's so embarrassing, so bad!')

Perhaps the single most striking attribute about Federer is his popularity as a human being. It's hard to find anyone with a bad word to say about him. Asked early in his career whether there was a maxim or proverb by which he lived his life, he said, 'It's nice to be important, but it's important to be nice.' He later said it wasn't quite a life-governing mantra, but it was a nice phrase he had heard and it was something he agreed with. Certainly, there are enough people who know him now and knew him as a boy who say that he lives by the motto. Madeleine Bärlocher, for instance, who ran the junior programme at Old Boys, describes him as 'a thoroughly nice guy. He's never looked down his nose at people. He's not made any big story, not tried to make himself popular. He's generous. And he has remained Roger.'

Marco Mordasini adds, 'There's nothing that you could spontaneously think of and say, "That's one of his downsides." His erratic behaviour on court isn't a problem any more. It hasn't disappeared; he's just got what causes it under control. He doesn't see the opponent as an enemy; he just wants to win the final point. He knows perfectly well that there are very few players who have the ability and weapons to beat him, but this superiority doesn't lead to him appearing arrogant or appearing like a diva on the court. He just radiates this sense of superiority, as if to influence the opponent in such a way that the opponent loses a sense of his own game. Churchill once said that you have to beat your opponent with his own weapons, and that applies to Roger.'

Such a personality is certainly a gift for tennis. 'He's a great model, a great promotion for our sport, says the ITF's president Francesco Ricci Bitti, 'and I think he's doing a great job. I think it's understandable that we want people like him to succeed.'

Federer is, however, only human and, despite all these compliments, his personality does include the flip side of some of his positive attributes. 'He always wants to be involved in decisions,' says Thomas Wirz of the *Basler Zeitung*. 'He's a very profound person who finds any incorrectnesses or unfairnesses hard to deal with, whether consciously or unconsciously, and thus, if anything isn't quite right, he can lose his thread, because he's basically a perfectionist.'

Federer's apparent lack of interest beyond tennis is sometimes held against him. He doesn't seem tremendously up-to-date with current affairs, and many were shocked at Wimbledon in 2005 when, at the height of the Live Aid initiative to raise money to alleviate poverty in the developing world, he admitted to not knowing who Bob Geldof was. It's possible that this is a poor example, and that Federer shouldn't be expected to know of a 1970s pop-singer-turned-charitable-icon, but it's generally accepted that his reading tastes are limited.

'I'm not convinced how intelligent he is,' said one unnamed observer from Basel. 'I've never been able to talk to him about anything other than tennis. Maybe that's my fault – maybe I haven't asked the right questions – but it's very difficult to find a subject he wants to talk about outside sport. I've never heard a statement from him about something other than sport that I've found of interest. I don't see the social component in Roger that I see in someone like Agassi.'

That particular view is not unique, but perhaps it's an unfair criticism. In June 2001, I conducted a lengthy interview with Federer in Halle for an article for a British newspaper and, after I'd asked my main questions, the interview developed partly into a casual chat. At one stage, the topic got on to South Africa and, in the course of the conversation, I asked him what he thought about the political situation there. He stopped in his tracks and said that at nineteen he couldn't be expected to make judgements about the politics of South Africa. For me, the most interesting aspect of that brief exchange wasn't that he didn't know enough about the subject to have an opinion (to admit you don't know something can be as much a sign of strength as of ignorance), but that I'd assumed he *would* have an opinion. Something about the assurance with which he talked about the country of his mother's childhood made me feel it was entirely logical to ask him about the political situation there. Maybe he is just waiting until he feels secure enough in his arguments before offering any opinions on matters of global importance. From my brief exchange with him, I suspect it won't be difficult for him to take an intelligent interest in something more meaningful than tennis when he decides to put his mind to it.

Another of his positive attributes that's coming back to haunt him as his international profile increases is his sense of politeness and helpfulness. In his early years on the tour, he said 'yes' to people very often but now finds that he can't oblige them as much as he used to because the demand for his time has become so much greater. A few people in Basel said it was sad that he seldom appears at Old Boys these days, especially as he came back on several occasions in the early part of his professional career. However, the club's president, Niki von Vary, says it is entirely understandable that his appearances are limited, given the fact that he can't turn up these days without some media interest following him.

He also has the 'problem' that life on the tour – and to some extent at home – is a seemingly constant stream of people fawning over him and offering him money to entice him to their events. People close to him have said he will never change, that his basic humanity is strong enough to withstand any temptation, but being plied with cash, admiration and adulation from all sides must nevertheless be a tough test. And when he turns down a reasonable request, it may be a sign of basic self-preservation.

Federer's increasing reluctance to play for Switzerland in the Davis Cup is also puzzling. It's legitimate to ask why he should prioritise the Davis Cup, especially when he doesn't know at the start of the year whether he will be playing two, three or four ties. He's right that the competition's format and calendar dates don't fall at a very opportune time for planning purposes, and he's a great believer in getting his tournament schedule right so as to reduce the risk of injuries. But there are two obvious reasons why he should play in the Davis Cup: firstly, he would be representing an entity greater than himself (his country) and, secondly, roughly every second tie would be a chance for him to play on home soil, when the only Swiss tournament that fits into his schedule is Basel – and he couldn't play there in 2004 and 2005 because of injury.

He won't give up on the Davis Cup completely. He needs to play a couple of ties and be 'in good standing with his national tennis association' if he wants to compete in the 2008 Olympics, which he certainly does. But when he chooses not to play for his country and appears in another tournament instead, it is not always clear what has motivated his decision.

When once asked what *he* thought were the negative sides of his character, Federer replied, 'I don't always listen to people because I'm dreaming too much, and I have to ask them to repeat what they say.'

And his mother said in an interview in 2005, 'I don't

have any major problems with him, only really that he is sometimes unpunctual.' It seems that a little of the indiscipline for which he was known in his days at Ecublens and Biel remains, but maybe that's reassuring.

Another question to consider is, given the intensity of competition in men's tennis, why should one man be able to dominate to such an extent? What makes Roger Federer so much more successful than his peers? Tennis coaches can describe what it is about his technique that makes his strokes so good, but they'll also confirm that it's not just his strokes that make him the best. He has a good, well-cared-for body and is deceptively quick around the court, but that's not an overwhelming advantage over the competition. And, much as the Wilson sporting-goods company would like people to believe that the racket Federer uses is the best, tennis isn't like motor racing, where the engineering that goes into the equipment effectively determines who can become world champion and who can't.

Federer is the best at what he does because he plays matches better than anyone else. But why? What is it in his mind that makes him so much better at what he does than even the best of the rest? One could break it down into various forms of psychological analysis – after all, tennis has seen its fair share of experts in the mind game. A cadre of qualified psychologists – of which Jim Loehr, of the Athletic Excellence Institute in Denver, is probably the best-known example – work one-to-one with players, while Timothy Gallwey, a tennis coach, published a book in 1974 entitled *The Inner Game of Tennis* that developed ways of allowing players to let their unconscious mind play matches, thus avoiding the conscious doubts and angst that can afflict the most gifted of players.

It wouldn't be appropriate here to go into a pseudo-psychoanalysis of Roger Federer's character, especially as the one time he has worked with a psychologist – back when he was seventeen years old – remains a very private matter about which little is known. But there are those who study the behaviour of people who are successful in their chosen field, and they can provide some enlightening analysis on what makes Roger Federer the best.

The technique of neuro-linguistic programming (NLP) was developed in California in the 1970s. It's designed to illustrate exactly why one person can perform a skill well while someone with the same basic attributes can excel at that same skill, and then to work out ways for others to emulate (or 'model') the successful person. The technique is used by numerous athletes in many sporting disciplines. One of NLP's leading authorities is Ian McDermott, who runs the British-based initiative International Teaching Seminars. He suggests looking closely at Federer's mentors. 'Children grow up modelling,' says McDermott, 'so Federer is going to have been influenced by his social environment – and one of the biggest influences he cites in his childhood was Peter Carter. Everyone who speaks about Carter talks of the inherent calmness of the man, and it's interesting that Federer's most significant breakthrough appears to have been his response to his outburst in Hamburg in 2001. If you look at the phrasing he uses when looking back on that event, he is clearly disassociating himself from his angry reaction to the way he played and saying he has to change the relationship he has with his own response. And in the back of his mind was this mentor who was calmness personified. Carter's calmness may be the most important thing Federer has modelled.

'Culturally, I think we've tended to become very critical of people who express strong anger or emotion after losing sporting contests. What Federer did in Hamburg was a clean response, as opposed to a muted reaction to defeat with the anger and emotions let out later and away from public view. But Federer obviously felt that this angry reaction wasn't working for him, so he learned how to change his response. Since then, he's operated a form of iron discipline, which we see as a calmness on court. These days there are just the occasional controlled explosions of anger or emotion when he threatens to boil over, like the time he blasted the ball away in his match at the Athens Olympics, or bursting into tears after winning the Australian Open – when incidentally Peter Carter's parents were present as his guests.'

With his experience of working with successful people in all walks of life, McDermott suggests that, having reached the top, Federer's biggest challenge might only now be beginning. 'To get to number one, Federer will have paid a price,' he says. 'A commitment to excellence when combined with a strong competitive streak tends to produce an extreme focus that can result in a certain unbalanced development, simply because you're so busy putting everything into the area that matters most to you. My experience of working with successful people is that very often the price they've paid is higher than it needed to be. Once they come to realise that, a rebalancing can take place, but this doesn't have to result in any diminishing of excellence. I can't help wondering whether Federer has paid a higher price than was necessary. Where has the fun-loving boy gone? Where is the prankster from the Basel tennis club who loved having fun on court but then found his concentration wandered? Perhaps if Federer were, say, to rediscover a little of his on-court sense of fun in matches while at the same time not losing the bite that makes him excel, he would reclaim a fuller sense of himself. That wouldn't just increase the accomplishment of his titles but would also make him much more attractive to fans, because people would have more of him to engage with. It would also reduce the risk of what happened with Pete Sampras happening to Federer – namely that, because he was so successful the same way, over and over again, people found that they had less to care about and even started to say he was boring.'

Only Federer himself can know how much fun he gets from being at the top of the tennis tree. But if he does ever find himself wondering where his next challenge lies and where he might go from here, maybe one option might be to attempt to move from being one of the world's most watchable tennis players because of the elegance of his strokes and his inherent good sportsmanship, to being one whom people care about as well as admire – and that might enhance his appeal even more.

Which begs the question: what does the future hold for Federer? As long as he remains fit and motivated, he is likely to play in about twenty-five further Grand Slam tournaments and two more Olympic Games, and in all of them he will start with a realistic chance of winning. The standard of international tennis is constantly improving, so he'll need to improve his own game if he wants to keep ahead, but the good news for him is that, while it's hard to pick holes in his game, there are a few areas where he still has room to get better.

For such a natural player, he still has something of a vulnerability on his volleys. It took him a long time to feel comfortable at the net, and then for a while he played his grass-court tennis by serving and volleying on every serve, first and second, but he has modified this approach, and has won his Wimbledon titles largely from the baseline. He is clearly one of the better volleyers on the tour, but, with modern racket technology making it much easier to hit passing shots than it was in the wood era, players now tend to go to the net either in an utterly commanding position to put away an easy volley or if they have immense trust in their volleys.

Federer is unlikely ever to volley as sweetly and athletically as Patrick Rafter, the Australian who was the best net player of his generation, but then Sampras never volleyed quite to that level, either, and his all-round game generally got the better of Rafter.

Nor is Federer the only top-class player to find he can lose confidence in his volleys mid-match and without warning; Martina Navratilova did so on several occasions but still managed to notch up eighteen Grand Slam singles titles. Federer has acknowledged that, as he gets older and loses a little speed, he will have to rely on his volleys more, so he might well need to build up his confidence now while he has such a dominant aura about him.

Another area in which he could improve, and which could be a key to winning the French Open, is his drop shots. He has said he lacks the clay-court specialist's ability to hit a dozen groundstrokes and then throw in a heavily disguised drop shot out of nowhere. And yet he has the technique, so it's just something he needs to work on.

Federer also still has a vulnerability when pushed wide. One could argue that everyone does, but the players who have beaten him on more than freakish occasions – particularly Nalbandian, Henman and Nadal – have used the angles to maximum effect, which suggests Federer still has room to develop a shot off both wings that can get him back into points when pushed out of his comfort zone. Part of the key here might lie in being able to add more topspin to his strokes when playing on slower surfaces.

Beyond his playing career, a wide range of options seems open to him. Unless he has a major disaster on the investments front, goes mad in his spending or is taken to the cleaners over a nasty divorce, he'll never need to work again, but of course such a bundle of energy will always require some occupation.

One possible future job is a television pundit, as he can talk sufficiently lucidly and has a good broadcast voice. He's an obvious Davis Cup captain for Switzerland, although probably not until a good five years after he's played his last match. He'd also be a valuable asset for any business looking for a global figure to front up a publicity campaign, and if he ever develops an interest in world affairs he could carve out a political role for himself, be it party-political, ambassadorial or for a non-governmental organisation (in the 1970s the US president Jimmy Carter asked Muhammad Ali to be a one-time envoy to Africa, and it would be easy to see Federer doing something similar).

There is another potential role for him in tennis. The 'seniors tour' circuit for big-name ex-professionals is currently thriving, and Federer would be a great catch. His combination of natural ability and the sense of fun that he has largely subjugated to allow him to keep his concentration means he could use the tour as his chance to have some real on-court amusement, given that the results don't matter so much. He could even take over the role that the Iranian player Mansour Bahrami currently plays – that of the seniors tour joker, who amuses crowds with trick shots and an irrepressible sense of fun. Whether Federer would want to is another matter, but there seems little doubt that he has the necessary attributes; he's just buried some of them for the purposes of being the best in the world.

Through this chapter, and indeed throughout this book, I've tried to identify the flaws in Federer's personality and game in order to paint a realistic picture of him. In truth, there are precious few of either, and there's no doubt he's a remarkable man and a great benefit to his sport. He exudes a calmness both on and off court that gives the impression of wisdom beyond his years, almost of an old soul who has an innate sense of what's really important and what can be discarded. And while the journalist Marco Mordasini might be correct in saying, 'You can't be as successful as he is without creating some envy,' it's astonishing how little envy Federer has created and how few enemies he has.

When I asked Seppli Kacovski, Federer's first coach and a man who has seen his fair share of real life and suffering, what he thought Federer's less attractive attributes might be, he replied, 'He must have his shadow sides, but I don't know them. I think he has everything he needs. He needs to be physical and competitive, so tennis gives him that. He has a sense of fun, and that is satisfied by people around him. He likes to make contact with people, so he gets them talking. He is basically fulfilled, and that is why he's the man he is.'

Bibliography

AS THIS IS the first full-length biography of Roger Federer, there is no obvious bibliography or recommendation for further reading. Much of the information in this book has come from my own personal experience, articles I've written for various publications and recordings of interviews and press conferences. Obviously, I cannot be everywhere, so a lot of information has come from other newspaper contributors, including fellow tennis journalists I have worked with and respect. I have tried to credit them at least once within the text.

That said, there are two short books that have been of considerable help to me. Roger Jaunin's French-language book *Roger Federer* (Favre/Le Matin, 2004, updated 2006) has been very helpful, particularly for its stories from the French-speaking part of Switzerland, while Freddy Widmer's German-language *Moments '05: Augenblicke mit Roger Federer* (*Basler Zeitung*, 2005) provided some of the details about Federer's background in Basel. Timothy Gallwey's *The Inner Game of Tennis* referred to in chapter 12 was published by Jonathan Cape in 1975.